Harlan Hoge Ballard

Hand-Book of the Saint Nicholas Agassiz Association

Harlan Hoge Ballard

Hand-Book of the Saint Nicholas Agassiz Association

ISBN/EAN: 9783337399009

Printed in Europe, USA, Canada, Australia, Japan

Cover: Foto ©Suzi / pixelio.de

More available books at **www.hansebooks.com**

HAND-BOOK

OF THE

ST. NICHOLAS
AGASSIZ ASSOCIATION.

BY HARLAN H. BALLARD,

PRINCIPAL OF LENOX ACADEMY.

Second Edition.

Bring us the airs of hills and forests,
The sweet aroma of birch and pine,
Give us a waft of the north-wind laden
With sweetbrier odors, and breath of kine!
Whittier.

LENOX, MASS.
PUBLISHED BY THE AUTHOR.
1884.

CHAPTER I.

THE ORIGIN.

The Agassiz Association, for the observation and study of natural objects, was founded in 1875 by the writer, in connection with a school which he was then teaching in Lenox, Mass. It was the outgrowth of a life-long love for Nature, and a belief that education is incomplete unless it include some practical knowledge of the common objects that surround us. For several years the little school society continued its work pleasantly and with profit. The President gradually came to the opinion (strengthened by reading an account of a somewhat similar, though far more limited, organization in Switzerland), that there might be other communities in which a like society would be welcomed, and several branch societies were organized. To test the matter more fully, having obtained the cordial co-operation of the editors of the St. Nich-olas, the leading publication for the young in the United States, a general invitation to unite in the work was published in 1880, in the November number of that magazine. It was substantially as follows :

THE INVITATION.

You must know that, across the ocean and over the Alps, the boys and girls of Switzerland have a bright idea. They have formed a society, and they have a badge. The badge is a spray of evergreen, and the society is a Natural History Society.

Once a year, in the spring time, when the sun has lifted the ice-curtain from the lakes, so that the fishes can look out, and the flowers can look in, the children from far and near come together for a meeting and a holiday. They are the boys and girls for a tramp. Their sturdy legs and long staves, their strong bodies and short dresses, their gay stockings and stout shoes prove that beyond a question.

The long golden hair of the girls, tightly braided and firmly knotted with gay ribbons, flashes brightly as they go clambering over rocks, leaping across rivulets, scrambling along glaciers, and climbing steep cliffs.

When the village schoolmaster, who usually leads these excursions, blows his horn, back come the children like laughing echoes, with baskets, pockets, boxes and bags full of the treasures of the wood.

Then they eat their dinner as we would take a picnic, and after that, spread out their trophies, and decide who has found the most, and who the rarest. They get the master to name them, if he can, and laugh in mischievious triumph when he fails.

With the lengthening shadows, the children return to their homes, and arrange their mosses, ferns and flowers, their pebbles, and beetles and butterflies, in cabinets, and declare, in their quaint accents, that they have had a glorious time. And have they not? The fresh, crisp air, the holiday, the sunshine, the picnic, the gathered specimens, and a teacher to tell them Latin names! No wonder they enjoy it. Would not you?

But on reflection we have all those things in this country, could we once bring them together in the right proportions. We have holidays enough—there are Saturdays. School-masters are as plentiful as schools. This is the same sun that shines on Switzerland, and it can find golden hair to kindle, without waiting for the sea to turn under it. Why, then, cannot we have a Natural History Society in America? In fact, we already have a little one, up here in these Berkshire Hills. And we enjoy it so thoroughly, and learn so much from it, that we wish it to grow larger.

Not many of you need be told why we have named our Society "THE AGASSIZ ASSOCIATION." There are few readers of *St. Nicholas* that have not heard something of the life and work of that famous man—so universally honored and beloved—Professor Louis Agassiz. In 1846 the great Naturalist left his native Switzerland, made America his home, accepted a Professorship at Harvard College, and built up the greatest school of Natural History in this country. Though one of the most learned, he was also one of the most devout and gentle of men.

Prof. Alexander Agassiz lends his cordial approval to our Society and its work, and has very kindly given us permission to use his father's name.

THE RESPONSE.

This invitation has met a response at once gratifying and unexpected. A very general interest in the study of Nature has been evinced by young and old. Classes or local " Chapters " have been formed in different towns, under the direction of the central organization, and where this has been impracticable, individuals have joined as corresponding members. Within three years and a half, more than seven thousand students have been aided, and six hundred and fifty local Scientific Societies established. Though originally planned as an aid to young people, the interest of the older ones has proved even greater, and we are gratified to find on our roll of membership the names of many fathers and mothers, teachers and professors. Several of our chapters are composed wholly of adults—many of old and young working together. " Family Chapters " are among our most successful branches.

SCHOOL SOCIETIES.

As the A. A. has become better known, it has found a wide field of usefulness in connection with schools, both private and public. Many teachers who have not been able to find a place for Natural Science in the ordinary school curriculum, and who have yet felt that their pupils should not grow up strangers to the flowers, trees, birds and butterflies, have been glad to devote an hour once a fortnight to the guidance of a meeting devoted to these studies. In almost every school may be found as many as six of the more intelligent boys and girls who will willingly spend an evening now and then in united study and discussion. The young are naturally fond of collecting. Most school committees will cheerfully grant the use of a room for the meetings, and many will even provide suitable cases for the specimens. No one need hesitate about organizing a local branch of our Society, from fear that his knowledge is too limited. We shall give full directions for beginning the work, and suggest several courses of study in a subsequent chapter. Many difficulties will be removed by correspondence with other classes that have surmounted the obstacles and passed the dangers which lie at the entrance of this, as of all other paths. The President of the A. A. is ready to render all the aid in his power, by referring you to the best books in the several departments, and by introducing you to one or more of the Specialists that have most generously volunteered their invaluable services to our Society.

SPECIAL CLASSES.

Among the pleasant features of the A. A. have been our special courses of study. These have been conducted by men high in their departments, and have always been free. Dr. Marcus E. Jones, of Salt Lake City, has taken a class through elementary Botany ; Prof. G. Howard Parker has directed a six months' course in Entomology ; Prof. E. L. French, of Wells College, has managed a very successful

course of botanical collecting, and exchange, and
Dr. Chas. Everett Warren, of Boston, has undertaken
to conduct a "Red Cross Class" through a course
of practical anatomy and physiology. All these
gentlemen have most generously volunteered their
services, and we cannot but hope that others will be
found to imitate their example of true philanthropy.

THE PLAN OF THE ASSOCIATION.

From this brief sketch of the origin and work of
the A. A., the purpose of its founder may be fairly
inferred. The association was designed to be an
extended free school of Natural Science—open to
persons of all ages and conditions. Local classes
or chapters were to be formed, quite independent of
each other, and of the President, except in so far as
by adopting a common name, and by a facility of
inter-correspondence and exchange, they might
render to each other mutual encouragement and
aid ; and by correspondence with the President, receive such guidance as he should be able to give
them.

It is mainly owing to the wide circulation and
powerful influence of *St. Nicholas* that the Association has attained its present vigor and extent. The
editors of that Magazine have afforded quite un-
usual means of making the Society known to others,
and of communicating regularly among ourselves.
As it has been our constant intention to have the A.
A. relieved from all machinery, politics and red
tape, and to have it resemble in a modest way, the
great school of Chautauqua, we have adopted the
following extremely simple Constitution, which gives
us just enough cohesion to stimulate an *esprit de*

corps, but leaves each class or chapter absolutely free from any jurisdiction whatever.

CONSTITUTION—(*As Amended.*)

Article 1. The name of this Society shall be THE AGASSIZ ASSOCIATION.

Art. 2. It shall be the object of this Association to collect, study, and preserve natural objects and facts.

Art. 3. The officer of this Association shall be a President, who shall perform the customary duties of such officer, and who, with the editors of *St. Nicholas*, may appoint his own successor.

Art. 4. New Chapters may be added with the consent of the President, provided that no such Chapter shall consist of less than four members.

Chapters shall be named from the towns in which they exist, and if there be more than one Chapter in a town, they shall be further distinguished by the letters of the alphabet.

Art. 5. Each Chapter may choose its own officers and make its own by-laws.

Art. 6. This Constitution may be amended by a three-fourths vote of the Association or its representatives.

Art. 7. The *St. Nicholas* Magazine shall be the official organ of communication between members and Chapters of the Association.

———

Of course Art. 7 lays no restriction on the correspondence, or other intercourse of Chapters, nor on the publication of local Chapter papers.

The wisdom of this plan of organization seems to be established by the rapid growth and increasing prosperity of the Society. First proposed to the public in 1880, it has now attained a membership of over 7,000, and consists of about 600 Chapters.

As may be seen by reference to the list of Chapters in another part of this book, these local societies are scattered throughout nearly all of the United States and Territories, Canada, England, Scotland, Ireland and South America.

ADVANTAGES.

The advantages which may result from the formation of a branch in the family or school, far outweigh the labor and time required. Habits of observation are formed ; valuable knowledge is acquired ; spontaneous study is secured ; health-giving rambles are taken ; the elements of parliamentary law are learned and practiced ; subjects for compositions are abundantly supplied ; power of debate is attained ; practice in letter-writing is necessitated ; valuable collections are made ; useful libraries are founded ; pleasant acquaintances are formed ; windows are opened into distant States through which we catch glimpses of scenery new to us ; we see various strange forms of animal and plant life, and the fossil records of the past ; and become acquainted with the modes of thought and expression which prevail outside our own homes. Correspondence with Chapters in different states is like the magical glass of the Arabian prince.

Sitting by our study-table we can see in every direction sturdy boys and graceful girls, searching eagerly for Nature's hidden treasures. We see them scouring the prairies of Kansas, climbing the foot hills of the Sierras ; discovering beautiful caves in the Rocky Mountains ; analyzing magnolia blossoms in Mississippi ; killing rattlesnakes on their own door-steps in Colorado ; studying geology in England ; gathering "edelweiss" from the slopes of the Alps ; wandering, by permit, through New York's Central Park ; spying out specimens from the mica mines of Vermont ; picking up tarantulas and scorpions in Texas ; searching for the flowers and insects of the Argentine Republic ; gathering algae and sea-shells on the coast of Florida ; growing wise in the paleontology of Iowa ; arranging the variously colored sands of the Mississippi river in curious bottles ; in Massachusetts, anxious to know whether "the *Limnanthemum* of our waters has roots ;" sending from Chicago to learn about the "center of buoyancy ;" holding field-meetings in Illinois ; celebrating the birthday of Professor Agassiz (May 28), in many States with a picnic and appropriate exercises ; giving entertainments and realizing "enough to buy a cabinet and have thirty dollars over to start a library" in Oregon ; making wonderful collections in Virginia ; enjoying the assistance and listening to the lectures of eminent scientists in Philadelphia ; enrolling scholars and teachers in Connecticut and Rhode Island ; determining to become professors in the District of Columbia ; writing fraternal messages from Canada; selecting quartz crystals from the hot springs of Arkansas ; discovering *geastrums* on Long Island, and everywhere learning to detect the beautiful in the common, and the wonderful in the before despised.

CHAPTER II.

HOW TO ORGANIZE A CHAPTER AND CONDUCT A MEETING. PARLIAMENTARY LAW. BY-LAWS.

We will now proceed to answer the most important and constant questions that come to us from day to day. Naturally the first inquiry is, "How can I form a Chapter of the A. A.?"

As four is the smallest number of members recognized as a "Chapter," the first thing to do is to find at least three persons besides yourself who are interested in the plan. Call a meeting and appoint a temporary chairman. Explain to your friends the purpose for which you have called them together, and make a motion to the effect that a chapter of the A. A. be organized. If this motion prevails, it will be well to have a committee appointed to draft your by-laws, or the rules by which your chapter is to be guided. After choosing this committee you may adjourn.

At the next meeting, hear and act upon the report of your committee, and elect your permanent officers. It will prove of great service to you to conduct your meetings, as far as may be, in accordance with parliamentary law. Your by-laws should contain an article stating what authority shall control you in this regard. You will find "Roberts' Rules of Order" an excellent and intelligible guide. If you have no book of rules, the following will be found to cover the principal points which may perplex you :

RULES OF ORDER.

1. A quorum of members is always required for the transaction of business, and in the absence of a special law, a majority of the members constitutes a quorum.

2. There is properly no business before the house until a member has been recognized by the chairman as having offered a motion.

3. It requires a two-thirds vote to suppress a question without permitting debate.

4. A motion to reconsider a question once decided can only be made by one who has voted affirmatively.

5. A rule adopted must be enforced by the chair without question.

6. Motions to lay on the table, and for the previous question are customary methods for disposing of questions and abridging debate.

7. Debate must be confined to the question, and personalities are out of order.

8. Motions which are undebatable, are the previous question ; to lay on or take from the table ; an objection to the consideration of any question ; an appeal relative to indecorum or violation of rule ; questions relative to the order of business, to the withdrawal of a motion, to reading papers or to suspending the rules ; and motions to adjourn, to fix the time to which to adjourn, or to postpone indefinitely. None of these can be amended except that to fix the time to which to adjourn. Precedence is given to motions in the following order ; and any motion, except to amend, can be made while one of a lower order is pending ; but none can supersede one of a higher order.

1. To fix the time to which to adjourn.
2. To adjourn. 3. A call for the order of the day.
4. To lay on the table. 5. The previous question.
6. To postpone to a certain time.
7. To commit, amend or postpone indefinitely.

BY-LAWS.

Very much of the comfort and harmony of your meetings will depend upon the wisdom of your by-laws. They should be simple, short and comprehensive, and should cover such points as what officers you will have, how long they shall hold office, what initiation fee you will require, how many members you will admit, what fines you will impose for absence, what duties shall devolve upon your officers and members, and what order of exercises you will follow in your meetings. The following schedule may prove serviceable as a suggestion :

1. The name of this society shall be, etc.
2. The officers shall be —.
3. The entrance fee shall be —.
4. The regular dues shall be —.
5. The order of exercises at our regular meetings shall be : *a.* Roll-call ; *b.* Minutes of last meeting ; *c.* Treasurer's report ; *d.* Report of corresponding secretary ; *e.* Reports of members on specimens, etc.; *f.* Miscellaneous business ; *g.* Adjournment.
6. New members may be elected at any regular meeting of the society, by ballot, and — adverse votes shall exclude.
7. The meetings of this society shall be conducted in accordance with ——, etc.

The second article should contain a clause limiting the time during which the various offices shall be held ; but considering the fact that the addresses of your President and Secretary are to be published in *St. Nicholas* and in the Hand Book, for the benefit of other chapters, those officers should be elected once for all, if possible. In any case you should take a P. O. Box, which may remain as the permanent address of your chapter through whatever official changes may occur.

In societies where members are of nearly the same age, the decision of the majority should be regarded as absolute, and be cheerfully agreed to by the minority. In family chapters, and those under the direction of a teacher, it is well to have a by-law giving the President the power of veto, and making a three-fourths vote necessary to pass a motion over his veto. Such branches may, if they choose, constitute simple classes, and remain entirely subject to the control of parent or teacher. The Constitution leaves each branch entirely free in these matters.

The first duty of your secretary, after having recorded the minutes of your meeting for organization, will be to send to the President of the Association an account of the formation of the chapter, containing the name, age, and special department of each member. Once in two months thereafter, a report of your progress will be expected. The nature of this report can best be learned by a study of those presented hereafter in this book. Should you, from any cause, disband, immediate notice should be sent to the President, so that other chapters may not address you in vain.

INDIVIDUAL MEMBERS.

It frequently happens that an individual wishes to join the A. A., but is not able to interest enough companions to form a chapter. To provide for such persons, we allow them to become corresponding members of the Central Association, at Lenox, on payment of an entrance fee of 50 cents. No subsequent dues are required, and for Chapters there is no expense, whatever, except the purchase of this book.

Those who join us as corresponding members, are expected to work in their chosen departments, and to send to the President, once a month, a concise report of their progress, modeled somewhat after the letters given later in the Hand-book. They enjoy all the privileges of charter members, except voting, and are at liberty to correspond and exchange with members of the regular chapters.

CHAPTER III.

A PLAN OF WORK.

The Presidents of those chapters that desire to study the scientific classification of the objects of Nature will do well to follow some such method as this : Consider, first, the three great kingdoms—Animal, Vegetable and Mineral. Let one meeting be devoted to the study of each as a kingdom. Let all the objects in your collection be classified so far as to determine regarding each, whether it belongs to the first, second or third of these kingdoms. Determine the same regarding a multitude of substances—as air, water, milk, sugar, amber, alcohol, ink, paper, steel, paint, silk, flannel, steam, smoke, coal, kerosene, vinegar, etc.

Next take up the branches into which the several kingdoms are subdivided. These are for Animals :

I.	Protozoa.	V.	Arthropoda.
II.	Cœlenterata.	VI.	Molluscoidea.
III.	Echinodermata.	VII.	Mollusca.
IV.	Vermes.	VIII.	Tunicata.
	IX. Vertebrata.		

Let these be carefully studied one by one, and thoroughly discussed, and illustrated by specimens, until any animal can readily be referred to its proper branch. If the books which contain this later classification are not at your command, you will do very well with the older divisions after Cuvier, viz.:

I.	Vertebrates.	III.	Mollusks.
II.	Articulates.	IV.	Radiates.
	V. Protozoans.		

2

These you will find in ordinary text-books, and I
may mention as peculiarly adapted to young people,
Tenney's Zoology, published by Scribner, Armstrong
& Co.

The divisions of the Vegetable kingdom are
given in Bessey's Botany, which is one of the best
and latest authorities on this subject; and in Gray's
various botanical works—the best of which for the
general student, is his " Lessons and Manual," or
for younger ones, "School and Field Botany."
These divisions and their further subdivisions should
be studied, as in the case of animals, carefully and
patiently. The Mineral kingdom is divided into
Metallic and Non-metallic substances, and these
again comprise objects which exhibit different de-
grees of hardness, fusibility, specific gravity, etc.,
regard being had also to their chemical compo-
sition and their peculiar forms of crystallization.
This is the most difficult kingdom for an unaided
student. Dana's "Mineralogy" is a good popular
guide, and Brush's " Determinative Mineralogy and
Blow-pipe Analysis" is an excellent manual for
more advanced students, while beginners cannot
do better than get some of the science primers
printed by Ginn & Heath, and mentioned later in
this book.

One object of this division and subdivision in the
several kingdoms is so to classify all natural objects that we may determine the precise name
of any specimen we may find. The more minute
the subdivision, the more difficult often becomes the
analysis. Thus, it is usually an easy matter to dis-
tinguish between an animal and a vegetable. It is
not difficult to determine whether we are examining

an insect or a worm. If we find an insect, we may
presently refer it to the *Lepidoptera*, and then to the
butterflies ; but when it comes to distinguishing between the various *vanessas*, with their curious punct-
uation marks, the matter grows more serious, and
we are compelled to obtain a book more restricted
in scope than a zoology, and, indeed, than most
entomologies.

As a result of this, it becomes necessary for him
that would accurately study any department of
Nature to limit himself early to a small field. One
will choose, for instance, *Dragon-flies*, and by de-
voting years to them will become a specialist and an
authority in that department. It is the tendency of
the times to produce specialists.

Many persons, however, are not willing to restrict
themselves to so narrow a field of study. They
prefer to range freely over mountain and along
stream, and having acquired the power to analyze a
flower or determine a mineral, they leave the one to
nod and smile on its dewy stem in undissected
beauty, and the other to sparkle in the sunlight, instead of crackling in the reducing flame of a com-
pound blow-pipe. Yet we must have strict scientists, and we honor the men who, for the sake of
expanding the world's knowledge, are willing to
confine their own researches to a narrow field.

For those, then, who are old enough to pursue a
systematic course, we have briefly outlined a plan
which may be followed in any department of Natural Science. It consists in first obtaining a general
view of the whole field, and then in learning its suc-
cessive subdivisions, until analysis is complete.

The rest of you, and especially you, my little folk

of ten years old and under, may, for the present,
leave the big books unopened, and the Latin names
unlearned. Watch the minnows dart about in the
crystal water; count the daisy flowers, and may
they prove oracles of joy; blow off the dandelion's
plumes to see if mother wants you; test your love
for butter by the glimmer of the buttercup beneath
your chins; find pretty pebbles by the brook and
keep them bright in glasses of water; gather brilliant
autumn leaves and press them for the days when
their colors will be in the sky; study the beautiful
crystals of the snow lightly falling on your sleeve
as you plod to school; learn to love the music of the
rain, and the singing of the wind, and the moaning
of the sea.

You may not discover many wonderful things—
or things that you will recognize as wonderful. But
St. Nicholas is a far traveler. If the boys and girls
in all the different places, gladdened by his visits,
were to tell each other about the common things in
each one's own vicinity, there would be wonder
enough, I am sure.

Yet you may find something altogether new. Did
not little Maggie Edward find a new fish for her
father? What? Never heard of Thomas Edward
—the dear old shoe-maker who used to make
"uppers" all day, and then lie all night in a hole in
a sand-bank, with his head and gun out, watching
for "beasts?" In that case, you would do well to
read the book called "The Scotch Naturalist," by
Samuel Smiles.

Nature must be studied out-of-doors. Natural
objects must be studied from the specimens themselves. The rocks must be broken open, the flowers

must be studied as they grow, and animals must be watched as they live freely in their own strange homes. Listen to quaint old Bernardin de St. Pierre, author of " Paul and Virginia :"

" Botanists mislead us. They must have magnifying glasses and scales in order to class the trees of a forest ! To show me the character of a flower, it is presented to me dry, discolored and spread out on the leaf of an herbary. Who can discover the queen of the flowers in a dried rose ? In order to its being an object at once of love and philosophy, it must be viewed when, issuing from the cleft of a humid rock, it shines on its native verdure, when the zephyr sways it, on a stem armed with thorns."

Nothing can take the place of personal contact with Nature. No great naturalist has learned his lessons from books.

Agassiz had learned more about fishes before he ever saw a fish-book, than he found in the book after he got it.

Audubon lived in the woods and learned the voices of all the birds, and could tell them also by their flight.

Gilbert White wrote charming letters about the swallows under his eaves, the cricket on his hearth, and the old tortoise that lived in his kitchen-garden.

W. W. Bailey braves the frosts of winter, and rambles by the icy brooks, or through the snow-carpeted aisles of the naked forest, to see what Nature does when summer is ended. Hear him :

" The pretty little stream is bordered by a fringe of white ice, under which we can see great bubbles press, squeezing themselves into very curious forms. The stream murmurs some pleasant story of the summer violets. On its still pools float leaf-gondo-las of curious patterns. Great fern-feathers, un-withered by the frost, droop over the brook, and velvety mosses cushion the shores."

These men understand Nature. They enter into the spirit of her mighty, throbbing life, and inter-pret the secrets of her wondrous love.

And if you have ever known what it is to feel a great love for the very earth, so that on some sunny day you have wandered off alone, and under the fragrant shade of an ancient pine, have thrown your-self upon her broad bosom, like a tired child; or if, when the wind was bending the long grass, you have lain among the daisies, like Robert Falconer, watch-ing your kite floating far up in the blue sky, and wondering what there is beyond the kite, and be-yond the sky; or if, on some dark day in December, when the gray clouds were skurrying across the sky, you have climbed a hill alone, and from a swaying perch in a leafless beech watched the drifting snow as it wrapped the world in ermine,—then you may believe that a portion of the spirit that animated Agassiz, and Edward, and Audubon, and White, and Wordsworth, has fallen upon you.

CHAPTER IV.

HOW TO MAKE A CABINET.

In " Rollo's Museum," a charming little book by
Jacob Abbot, we read that Jonas made an excellent
cabinet for Rollo, from a large packing-box.   He
stood it on end, fitted it with shelves, and closed it
by doors attached by means of leather hinges, and
fastened by a wooden button.   Such a cabinet neatly
finished, looks very well, and costs almost nothing.
To those who would like to try their hands at something a little more elegant, we offer the following
simple design:

The picture
shows the cabinet
complete, and the
plan following it is
drawn so that ev-
ery measurement
in it is one-six-
teenth of the cor-
responding meas-
urement in the
finished cabinet.
No nails are used.
Wood of light
color looks well; chestnut is easily worked.   The
ends of the top and bottom are mortised into the
sides.   Close to the side boards, holes are bored
through the projecting parts of the tenons ; and
wedges are inserted and hammered tight.

The frames of the doors are doweled at the corners, each joint being made by boring a hole through one piece into the next, and inserting a dowel coated with glue. The short dotted lines in the plan help to explain this. The glass should not be set with putty, but with narrow strips, beading, or rattan, fastened with brads or " needle points." Butt-hinges may be used, with ornamental hinge-plates set outside, as shown. Hook one door to the shelf, and it will hold the other door shut.

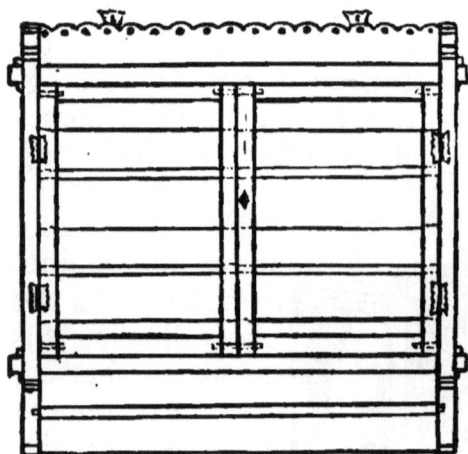

The shelves may be made with raised edges, like trays,— the front rims are not shown in the picture. These edges will keep the contents from rolling off when the trays are taken out. The shelves slope forward to show the specimens to better advantage; and they rest on dowels let into auger-holes in the side boards. To prevent them from slipping, pegs are set in them underneath, resting against the backs of the forward dowels. The shelves may be put in flat, and may rest on screw eyes screwed into the sides of the cabinet,

Metal ears are set on the back, projecting above the top, for hanging the cabinet; in addition, it is well to drive a screw from the inside through the back into a stud in the wall.

The scalloping at the top of the back may be done

with a fret-saw. The hole in the center of each scallop is bored right through. The ornamental lines across the sides are made with a gouge, and should be covered with two coats of white shellac varnish. Those skilled in fret-sawing may like to set in the top the letters 𝔄. 𝔄., in Old English text. If you are puzzled over any of the details, the nearest cabinet maker will give you a friendly hint.

Many chapters wishing something still more elaborate, have given various sorts of entertainments, and earned money to buy them, and in many cases the school authorities have generously furnished our young friends with cabinets, and rendered them other substantial aid.

One of the most desirable kinds of cabinet, is made like a shallow show-case, and the top is covered with a glass door which may be lifted up. In a case for insects, this top may be tightly fastened down by means of thumbscrews, and may be rendered airtight by the interposition of a strip of rubber.

CHAPTER V.

[*By the courtesy of Prof. Gray, and the Publishers, most of these hints on collecting plants, are taken from Gray's Lessons in Botany: Ivison, Blakeman, Taylor & Co., N. Y.*]

HOW TO COLLECT SPECIMENS AND MAKE AN HERBARIUM.

For collecting specimens the needful things are a large *knife*, strong enough to be used for digging up bulbs, small rootstocks, and the like, as well as for cutting woody branches; and a *botanical box*, or a *portfolio*, for holding specimens which are to be carried to any distance.

It is well to have both. The *botanical box* is most useful for holding specimens which are to be examined fresh. It is made of tin, in shape like a candle-box, only flatter, or the smaller sizes like an English sandwich-case; the lid opening for nearly the whole length of one side of the box. Any portable tin box of convenient size, and capable of holding specimens a foot or fifteen inches long, will answer the purpose. The box should shut close, so that the specimens may not wilt: then it will keep leafy branches and most flowers perfectly fresh for a day or two, especially if slightly moistened.

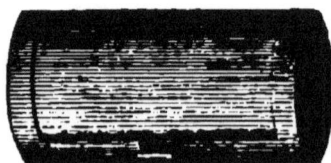

The *portfolio* should be a pretty strong one, from a foot to twenty inches long, and from nine to eleven inches wide, and fastening with tape, or (which is better) by a leathern strap and buckle at the side. It should contain a quantity of sheets of thin and smooth, unsized paper; the poorest print-ing-paper and grocers' tea-paper are very good for the purpose. The specimens as soon as gathered are to be separately laid in a folded sheet, and kept under moderate pressure in the closed portfolio.

Botanical specimens should be either in flower or in fruit. In the case of herbs, the same spec-imen will often exhibit the two; and both should by all means be secured whenever it is possible. Of small herbs, especially annuals, the whole plant, root and all, should be taken for a specimen. Of larger ones branches will suffice, with some of the leaves from near the root. Euough of the root or subter-ranean part of the plant should be collected to show whether the plant is an annual, biennial or peren-nial. Thick roots, bulbs, tubers, or branches of specimens intended to be preserved, should be thinned with a knife, or cut into slices lengthwise.

For drying specimens a good supply of soft and unsized paper—the more bibulous the better—is wanted; and some convenient means of applying pressure. All that is requisite to make good dried botanical specimens is, to dry them as rapidly as possible between many thicknesses of paper to ab-sorb their moisture, under as much pressure as can be given without crushing the more delicate parts. This pressure may be given by a botanical press, of which various forms have been contrived; or by weights placed upon a board,—from forty to eighty or a hundred pounds, according to the quantity of specimens drying at the time. For use while trav-eling, a good portable press may be made of thick binders' boards for the sides, holding the drying paper, and the pressure may be applied by a cord, or, much better, by strong straps with buckles.

For drying paper, the softer and smoother sorts of cheap wrapping-paper answer very well. This paper may be made up into *driers*, each of a dozen sheets or less, according to the thickness, lightly stitched together. Specimens to be dried should be put into the press as soon as possible after gathering. If collected in a portfolio, the more delicate plants should not be disturbed, but the sheets that hold them should one by one be transferred from the portfolio to the press. Specimens brought home in the botanical box must be laid in a folded sheet of the same thin, smooth, and soft paper used in the portfolio; and these sheets are to hold the plants until they are dry. They are to be at once laid in between the driers, and the whole put under pressure. Every day (or at first even twice a day would be well), the specimens, left undisturbed in their sheets, are to be shifted into well-dried fresh driers, and the pressure renewed, while the moist sheets are spread out to dry, that they may take their turn again at the next shifting. This course must be continued until the specimens are no longer moist to the touch,—which for most plants requires about a week: then they may be transferred to the sheets of paper in which they are to be preserved. If a great abundance of drying paper is to be used, it is not necessary to change the sheets every day, after the first day or two.

Herbarium. The botanist's collection of dried specimens, ticketed with their names, place, and time of collection, and systematically arranged under their genera, orders, &c., forms a *Hortus Siccus* or *Herbarium.* It comprises not only the specimens which the proprietor has himself collected, but those which he acquires through friendly exchanges with distant botanists, or in other ways. The specimens of an herbarium may be kept in folded sheets of neat, and rather thick, white paper; or they may be fastened on half sheets of such paper, either by slips of gummed paper, or by glue applied to the specimens themselves. Each sheet should be appropriated to one species; two or more different plants should never be attached to the same sheet. The generic and specific name of the plant should be added to the lower right-hand corner, either written on the sheet, or on a ticket pasted down at that corner; and the time of collection, the locality, the color of the flowers, and any other information which the specimens themselves do not afford, should be duly recorded upon the sheet or the ticket. The sheets of the herbarium should all be of exactly the same dimensions. The herbarium of Linnæus is on paper of the common foolscap size, about eleven inches long and seven wide. But this is too small for an herbarium of any magnitude. Sixteen and a half inches by ten and a half, or eleven and a half inches, is an approved size.

The sheets containing the species of each genus are to be placed in *genus-covers*, made of a full sheet of thick, colored paper (such as the strongest Manilla-hemp paper), which fold to the same dimensions as the species-sheet; and the name of the genus is to be written on one of the lower corners. These are to be arranged under the orders to which they belong, and the whole kept in closed cases or cabinets, either laid flat in compartments, like large "pigeon-holes," or else placed in thick portfolios, arranged like folio volumes, and having the names of the orders lettered on the back.

It may not be out of place, in connection with rules for preserving plants, to give the following method of preparing specimens of wood for the cabinet: Cut boards five by eight inches and a quarter of an inch thick. Season, and plane smooth. Varnish one-half. Then cut from a sapling, two or three inches in diameter, some pieces one-quarter of an inch thick. Saw these in a square miter-box.

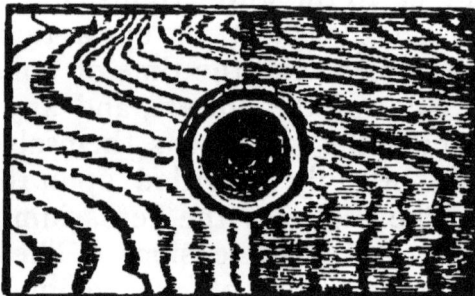

SPECIMEN OF WOOD.

Saw off several, as some may warp or split. In summer, the pieces will season without a fire. In winter, a fire is needed, but the wood should not be put too near it. When the end sections are seasoned, smooth one side carefully with a rasp, so as not to mar the bark. Finish with fine sand-paper. Polish, oil, or varnish, being careful not to varnish the bark. When dry, fasten with small screws, from the back, to the center of the boards previously described.

CHAPTER VI.

HOW TO COLLECT AND PRESERVE SEA-WEED.

Louisa Lane Clarke, in "*Common Sea-weeds,*" gives the following suggestions, which are evidently the fruit of experience. Even in these minor details she reveals her true love of nature. "We dabble in the cool, clear tide-pools, and scarcely know what we take up; there is a world of life in each. The speckled prawn is balancing himself, and waving to and fro his sensitive feelers, springing away under the rich foliage that conceals his hiding-place; and the small Blenny darts like a lightning-flash from cranny to crevice, the fear and the dread of man upon it. On the green *Ulva* creeps the lovely little slug—a bright green spotted with white —called *Acteon viridis,* and on darker sea-weeds the great purplish Sea-hare. Sea-spiders lurk amid the coralline; and as we gather a bunch of sea-weed, we shake out dozens of a pretty little snail called *Rissoa,* besides gathering, if we please, bright yellow *Nerits,* the commonest sea-snail of our coast. All these force themselves on the notice of the sea-weed gatherer, as we scramble over the rocks, and pause to consider where we shall begin.

I advise taking a little of everything—not much, for they so soon spoil in waiting to be mounted— and naming each specimen as it is decided by reference to your manual. If you have time to spare, be content to press and arrange the weeds mentioned as belonging to the first tide-pools. If you have but a day for a sea-side holiday, go down to the lowest ebb of the tide, in hopes of the best *red* sea-weeds, and work back to the commoner, but still beautiful, green sea-weeds, *Ulva* and *Cladophoræ.*

Suppose now, that we have made our search, and have brought home a tangled mass of olive, red and green sea-weeds.

We get some soup-plates, fresh water, a bit of alum, some camel-hair pencils, and *I* use needles, mounted on lucifer matches, to assist in disentangling the mass.

Of course we are prepared with paper cut into large and small squares; and as much of the beauty of the specimens depends on the quality of the paper, it should be fine, and at the same time stout, almost as good as drawing paper.

Now float a piece of weed in fresh water; if very dirty or sandy, wash it first, and in renewed water float it on a piece of paper supported by your left hand, whilst with your right hand you arrange the plant in a natural manner, using a mounted needle or porcupine-quill, and thinning out the superabundant branches with a fine pointed pair of scissors. When the specimen is placed as you like it, cautiously raise the paper that the position of the plant be not altered, and let it rest somewhere with sloping inclination, that the moisture may run off whilst other specimens are treated in the same way.

Do not leave them long thus, for they must be pressed before the paper is dry.

A convenient traveling press consists of two pieces of deal board about two feet long and one foot wide, a couple of quires of whity-brown paper, and a double strap. Lay blotting paper between the coarser paper, and you can strap them closely, and carry your sea-weed very safely in your hand.

In drying them, you must have old linen or fine muslin, old and soft, to lay upon the weed and prevent its sticking to the upper paper; but do not leave it beyond a day or so, lest it leave chequered marks upon the surface of the weed, especially those with broad fronds, like *Delesseria*.

Experience will give the best lessons. Some sea-weeds, such as *Melogloia*, which are glutinous, must not be pressed at all, but laid out to dry, and when perfectly so, then moisten the *under* side of the paper, and give a gentle pressure only.

Others will not adhere to paper, and therefore, when dry, brush them over with a little isinglass dissolved in gin (laid on warm,) and they will then be fixed closely to the cardboard or paper.

Another preparation is: one ounce oil of turpentine, in which some gum mastic the size of a nutmeg has been dissolved. This gives a gloss to the specimen, and helps to preserve the color.

You must change the blotting paper and muslin at least twice during the process of drying larger sea-weeds; the smaller ones will be ready in a couple of days for the album, on the second day giving heavy pressure by stones and weights besides the strap.

3

CHAPTER VII.

HOW TO COLLECT, STUDY AND PRESERVE INSECTS.

Of the seven thousand members of the Agassiz Association, more have expressed a preference for the study of entomology than for almost any other branch. Curiously enough, the girls seem to be quite as fond of insects as the boys are. It is not difficult to account for this preference. The many-hued wings of butterflies flashing in the sun, the metallic gleam of beetles, the feathery grace and rich coloring of moths, the dreamy pinions of drag-on-flies, the excitement of the chase, and above all, the mysterious and symbolic changes which attend insect-life, shed a bright fascination about insect-study.

Attracted by this light our boys and girls are fluttering about the homes of bugs and beetles very much in the same manner that bugs and beetles flutter about the lights in our human habitations. Let me, then, hasten to answer the three questions which are puzzling so many of our correspondents: How catch? how kill? how keep? By far the best way to catch a butterfly is to find a caterpillar; keep him in a glass box; feed him with leaves of the plant on which you found him; and watch him day by day, as he changes his various garments, "spins himself up" till he bursts or perforates his cerements and unrolls his wings, with every painted shingle in its place, his "feathers" quite unruffled on his head and his six legs under him in unmutilated entireness. Full directions for raising insects, making glass cases, etc., are contained in a little book called "Insect Lives," published at a dollar by Robert Clarke, Cincinnati, Ohio.

In addition to this method of capture, you will need a light gauze net. Any boy can make one of these in half an hour. Get three-fourths of a yard of silk veiling; ask Mother to make a bag of it, with a hem around the top wide enough to run a pipe-stem through; pass a thick wire through this and bend it into the shape required; fasten the ends of this wire to a light stick, five or six feet long, and your net is made. A piece of a bamboo fishing rod makes a good handle. You may also need a stouter net for beating about in the bushes.

A third method of capturing moths is that of painting trees with a mixture of rum, beer and sugar. This is done in the early evening, and later, lantern in hand, you go about from tree to tree and tap into your net the insects stupefied by the sweet but fatal sirup.

A very successful lure may be formed by enclosing a female moth, alive, in a box covered with gauze. Frequently a large number of moths may be taken in a single evening as they hover about the imprisoned insect.

For the capture and conveyance of beetles, etc., a good supply of pill-boxes and vials of various sizes may be carried in the pockets. Small forceps are convenient for picking up spiders, which, however, are not now classed with true insects.

These smaller insects may be dropped at once into a bottle of alcohol, and cared for on reaching home.

Butterflies are easily killed by a sudden and strong

compression of the thorax. They are best carried home by folding the wings back and enclosing them in little three-cornered envelopes, not glued, but merely folded over them.

·A vial of chloroform with a camel's hair brush attached to the inside of its rubber cork, is convenient. A drop on the head of an insect will render it insensible, and it may be pinned into your collecting box. But the best plan for killing large insects is the *Cyanide jar*.

Take a wide-mouthed candy jar; get your druggist to lay four or five pieces of cyanide of potassium, as large as walnuts, in it, and cover them with a layer of sawdust. Over this fit a piece of writing paper. Then pour over all half an inch of liquid plaster of Paris. This will quickly harden, forming a smooth floor, on which any insect when dropped, will quickly and quietly pass away.

The jar must be labeled poison, and must be kept closed with an air-tight cover.

A collecting case can be made of any light, shallow box, by lining it with cork, and affixing straps by which it may be slung around the neck. Compartments may be made in it, for the cyanide and chloroform bottles, for forceps, insect pins, envelopes, etc. Having got your insects home, they must be carefully mounted. You should have several 'setting-boards.' These are simply thin boards, grooved at intervals so as to admit the bodies of different sized moths and butterflies, in such a way that their wings may be flat on the board. Strips of cork may be glued along the bottom of the grooves to receive the pins.

Pin your specimens in a groove of proper depth,

and spread his wings carefully with your forceps or
needles set in wooden handles.

Fasten them by laying strips of glass over them,
or by pinning strips of paper across them. They
should be allowed to dry for a week or two according to size. The bodies of large lepidopera should
be brushed with a solution of corrosive sublimate,
one-half drachm; arsenic, four grains; alcohol, one-
half pint. This is of course very poisonous, and
*you should get some older friend to prepare and apply
it for you.*

Your insects may now be pinned into cedar cases,
made air-tight, and guarded by lumps of camphor
gum. In addition to these precautions, all specimens should be subjected to a rigid quarantine of a
month before being transferred to the collection.
Even then, the cases must be carefully examined
every month, and any indications of danger must
be regarded. If such appear, pour a few drops of
chloroform into the case, and close the cover. This
will drive the destructive creatures into sight from
crack and cranny. Kill them, preserving one or two
for specimens, and renew your previous precautions.
A simpler and as effectual a method is to give your
mounted insects, cases and all, a thorough baking
in the oven, but this also requires great care, as the
heat will spoil some kinds.

Mr. E. S. Morse gives probably the best device
for arranging an insect box for the cabinet. It consists of a light wooden frame like a slate frame, with
paper stretched upon the upper and lower surfaces.
Dampen the paper and glue it to the frame, and
when the paper dries, it will contract and become as
tight as a drum head. Inside the box upon two

sides fasten cleats and let their top edges be about a quarter of an inch above the bottom. Rest the paper-covered frame upon these cleats. The bottom of the box should be covered with soft pine to receive the points of the pins. The space under the frame should be dusted with snuff and camphor to keep out insects.

But, after having tried many methods, I have been best pleased with the appearance of insects that I have set up on separate, papered blocks of wood, such as are used for minerals. Indeed I know of no way of showing any of the smaller specimens, such as shells, bird's eggs, insects, fossils, &c., to so good advantage as to set each by itself on a white block of suitable size. For young entomologists, I know of no better book, on the whole, than " Harris on Insects injurious to Vegetation."

I will add for the benefit of our young entomologists a few hints on methods of observation furnished by Prof. G. Howard Parker of Cambridge, and Prof. Asa Packard, Jr., of Providence. Every naturalist should have a pocket note-book always with him, and make careful entries of such points as are here indicated. Suppose, for example, you take first, butterflies and moths. It would be an excellent plan to prepare a paper, in which you might:

1. Give a brief but clear description of the *order*. (Lepidoptera.

2. Give a careful report of your own observations on any one species of the order. In this report should be included:

A. *Description* of the insect, accurate as may be, and, if possible, accompanied by drawings, however rude.

[This description should be made as follows:

a. If a moth or butterfly, note: 1st. The *form of the antennæ*, whether pectinated or simply hairy or spindle-shaped. 2d. The form and size of palpi and length of tongue. 3d. Wings: 1st pair, form, shape of costal, apex, outer edge veins. 2d pair same. 4th. Markings on wings. 5th. Feet, spurs.

b. If a caterpillar, note: 1st. Form of head, wider or narrower than segment next. 2d. Dorsal, subdorsal, and lateral stripes. 3d. Position of tubercles, warts, or spines, and spots. 4th. Spiraculaı line. 5th. Supra-anal plate; its form and markings. 6th. Number of abdominal legs and form of last pair.

c. Difference in coloration of the sexes; varieties observed; probable cause of such variation, such as differences of food. location, and time of year.]

B. *Habits.*—Date of appearance and disappearance of the *perfect insect:* number of annual broods; localities most favorable, etc.

C. *Transformations.*—1. The egg: description, sketch, duration of this stage; where and how deposited by the female. 2. Larva: number of molts, and changes noticed in these molts; duration of each molt, and entire time consumed in this stage; food-plants of the larva; drawings. 3. Chrysalis: description; methods of protection and fastening; duration of this stage; special observations. 4. Parasites observed during these stages (ichneumons, chalcids, etc.)

d. Concluding remarks, with notes drawn from various works on the subject, and a list of such references.

Having thus worked up a few species of Lepidoptera, you might, to advantage, take up successively the other orders, Hymenoptera, Coleoptera, Neuroptera, etc., treating them in the same way, and concluding the course by a careful study of "Insects as a Class." Then you can return to your favorite order or family, and carry on your special researches and observations, minutely and intelligently.

We add the following Department directions for sending insects by mail :

"All inquiries about insects, injurious or otherwise, should be accompanied by specimens, the more the better. Such specimens, if dead, should be packed in some soft, material, as cotton or wool. and inclosed in some stout tin or wooden box. They will come by mail for one cent per ounce. *Insects should never be inclosed loose in the letter.* Whenever possible, larvæ (*i. e.* grubs, caterpillars, maggots, etc.) should be packed alive in some tight tin box,—the tighter the better, as air-holes are not needed,—along with a supply of their appropriate food sufficient to last them on their journey; otherwise, they generally die on the road and shrivel up. Send as full an account as possible of the habits of the insect respecting which you desire information; for example, what plant or plants it infests; whether it destroys the leaves, the buds, the twigs, or the stem; how long it has been known to you; what amount of damage it has done, etc. Such particulars are often not only of high scientific interest, but of great practical importance. In sending soft insects or larvæ that have been killed in alcohol, they should be packed in cotton saturated with alcohol. In sending pinned or mounted insects, always pin them securely in a box to be inclosed in a larger box. the space between the two boxes to be packed with some soft or elastic material, to prevent too violent jarring. *Packages should be marked with the name of the sender."*

CHAPTER VIII.

HOW TO COLLECT AND PRESERVE BIRDS.

It is not worth while to make a collection of mounted birds. This requires too much time and too much room. But, especially, skins are better and more convenient for study than mounted birds. Skins may be kept in a cabinet with tightly fitting drawers, with plenty of camphor, or insect powder. The best arm for general purposes is the double-barreled, breech-loading shot-gun. Three-fourths of your cartridges should contain small charges of mustard-seed shot, and the remainder, No. 8 and No. 4. You can indicate the kind of shot in each shell by having numbers on your shot-wads. Early morning and late evening are the best hours, and well-watered and wooded spots the best places for collecting. As each specimen is secured, it must be carefully cleansed and smoothed. Plug mouth, nostrils, vent, and shot-holes with cotton, and thrust the bird head first into a paper cone, to keep the plumage from injury.

A fish basket is excellent to carry the birds home. Before skinning, each bird should be measured to determine the total length, and the spread of wings. Note, also, the color of the eyes, bill, and feet, as they may fade. Enter all these memoranda in a note-book, and also on the specimen label. Add also date of capture, sex, locality, name of collector, etc., etc.

SKINNING.

See that throat, nostrils, and wounds are well plugged with cotton, and fasten some also around the bill. Should any blood get on the feathers remove it at once with a damp sponge, and dry with plaster of Paris. Lay the bird on its back, separate the breast feathers right and left, cut from the breast bone to the vent (not cutting the flesh), and raise the skin carefully on each side as far as the legs. Cut off the legs at the knee joints, inside the skin, and afterward skin down to the tarsus, scraping the flesh from the shin bone, but leaving that bone in place. Next skin around the coccyx, or tail bones, and cut off the coccyx inside the skin, leaving enough flesh to hold the feathers. Hang the bird head downward, by a hook inserted in the exposed stump of the rump, and carefully strip off the skin by turning it back like a glove, as far as the wings ; cut off the wings, inside the skin, at shoulder joint. Skin the wing bones, and scrape the flesh from them, as from the legs. Skin over the head to the bill, taking especial care not to stretch the skin. The skin above the ears and eyes will have to be detached by cutting. The eyes must now be picked out, and the entire base of the skull removed, together with the brain, and the flesh between the jaws. If the head is too large to be skinned in this way, an incision must be made under the throat, which can afterward be sewed. The skin is now inside out. Powder with arsenic, or soap with arsenic soap, turn it right side out, and allow it to become perfectly dry. Smooth the plumage, set the bones of legs. and wings into proper position, and the bird is ready for stuffing. A pellet of cotton, as large as the bird's eye, should be passed into the skin and pressed into each socket. Over this adjust the eyelids. Wrap a little cotton around the leg bones of large birds. Insert a cylinder of cotton, rather smaller than the neck, into the neck. Mould the body-stuffing into a mass, rather smaller than the bird's body. Bring the edges of the skin nicely together over this, and the stuffing is completed. Fold the wings neatly, adjust the head and neck, bring the feet together, and press the bird into the proper shape. The usual fault is too much stuffing, especially between the shoulders. For mounting specimens some knowledge of comparative anatomy is desirable. The habits of each bird must be carefully studied, as well as its peculiar manner of sitting, standing, holding the head, etc. The art of taxidermy should be carefully studied, from such manuals as Swainson's, Brown's, or Sylvester's. Of the other two we cannot speak from observation, but Captain Brown's book, published at $1.50, by Putnam & Co., of N. Y., is excellent and very full. We are indebted for much of the information contained in this chapter to Professor Stearns' excellent "Bird Life," and to the kindness of the Manhattan Chaper of the A. A.

CHAPTER IX.

HOW TO COLLECT AND ARRANGE MINERALS.

Few directions are necessary. Minerals do not have to be pursued over brier and brake as butterflies, nor are they perishable in their nature. They have not to be pressed nor kept in alcohol. You will need a strong geologist's hammer, a sharp-pointed iron, to pry crystals from the rocks, and a stout bag to carry home your specimens. For the analysis of minerals you will need a simple blow-pipe, a small steel hammer and anvil, a magnet, a knife, a pair of platinum forceps, a clay-pipe, and a few chemicals, all of which are described in Brush's Determinative Mineralogy and Blow-pipe Analysis. Unless, however, you have a competent guide at your elbow, we do not advise you to begin your studies in so difficult a manner. I know of no better plan than to procure from Ginn & Heath, W. O. Crosby's little 35 ct. book, "Common Minerals and Rocks," with the accompanying set of labeled specimens, and make yourself master of both. Fortunately the number of distinct types of *common* minerals is small, and one may easily become familiar with them. Your specimens should be carefully labeled, either by numbers referring to a catalogue, or by cards containing the name, date, locality, etc. Specimens of minerals will not bear huddling together Their appearance is greatly enhanced by placing each by itself on a neat block of wood painted white, or papered. In making a collection of minerals, as in all other departments, bear in mind Prof. Agassiz's excellent advice to the effect that the most valuable work a society can do, is to make a complete collection and thorough study of the specimens found near its own home. Do not let visions of sparkling crystals or gleaming ores from distant states blind you to the value and importance of the sand-stone under your feet, the slate on your roof, the coal in your cellar, or the pebbles by the brook.

CHAPTER X.

WHAT TO DO IN WINTER AND IN THE CITY.

No questions have been more frequently repeated. None can be more easily answered.

One of the things which those who live in cities can do, is to make drawings of snow-crystals to exchange for specimens more easily found in the country. Catch the crystals, as they fall, on a dark cloth. Look at them through a magnifying glass, if you have one, and draw as well as you can from memory.

The drawings should be made of a uniform diameter of half an inch. Six drawings may be made nicely on a card as large as a postal card. For convenience in exchanging, we all may make them of the same size and arrange them in the same way, as follows:

SNOW CRYSTALS. DRAWN BY CORWIN LINSON.

To have these crystal pictures valuable, we must notice the conditions which prevail as the snow falls. Look at the thermometer and barometer, and note the strength of the wind, as well as the date. Attention to these details will enable us to decide whether or not snow-crystals vary in shape with heat and cold and density of air, etc.

Another thing you of the city can do, is to suspend seeds over water in bottles, and study the growth of different plants as the tiny leaves unroll. Make neat cases also for insects, or minerals, and exchange them for specimens. Collect specimens of veneers from cabinet and piano shops, and prepare them for exchange. Nearly all the grains, and nuts, and spices, and fabrics, and seeds, and barks, and woods, and metals, can be found in city shops, and for these you can readily get anything you may wish from the country. Again, many of you have books or pictures on subjects of natural history which are old to you, but which some member of the Association would be very thankful to get. These, also, can be exchanged.

Besides these things, we need only mention birds'-nests abandoned in leafless trees, cocoons suspended from bushes and tucked away under fence-rails, beetles burrowing in old stumps, sections of wood and bark, cones and buds, to show that there is plenty of out-door work, even in winter ; while, indoors, cabinets are to be built, specimens determined, labeled, and arranged, philosophical experiments performed, books read, letters written, exchanges made.

Many of our members capture caterpillars and other insects in the fall, and keep them during the winter, watching their curious habits, and wonderful transformations, as is detailed in the following bright letter :

"DEAR MR. BALLARD: I have been reading 'Insect Lives.' It is the nicest book I have ever read. I could read a whole library full of books just like that. I am getting on famously with my collection. But one of my caterpillars does act so funny. It is the caterpillar of that moth —the '*Polyphemus*,' is it? I found him two days ago, and put him in my box. He seemed very sluggish. If I turned him over, he would very slowly turn himself over back again; but I thought perhaps he was going to change his skin, or something like that. The next afternoon I looked at him, and there were hundreds of little worms coming out of holes in his skin (horrid things!) I was going to burn him up, but decided to wait and see what would come of it. The next morning nearly all of them had changed into little grayish-brown cocoons, and tumbled off, leaving tiny holes in his skin, and now he is twisting about like a good fellow. ANNIE BOSWORTH."

The sequel to this tragedy was told in a subsequent letter from the same excellent observer :

"My poor worm died the day after I wrote you, and a day or two after the little rice-houses began to open, and hundreds of tiny flies came out from them, but I threw them away in disgust."

CHAPTER XI.

EXCHANGING.

One of the pleasantest features of the A. A. is the exchange of specimens between members. Some hints may be helpful. When you have duplicates which you wish to exchange, decide as nearly as possible what you wish in return. Send your request, tersely written, to the President. It will appear in *St. Nicholas* in either two or three months. The magazine is printed sometime before it is issued, so that you must send any notice at least two months before you wish to see it in print. In preparing packages for the mail, be sure that you enclose the specimens in a box sufficiently strong to withstand the frequent concussions of the way, and so securely wrapped and tied that it shall not become undone. About one-third of the packages received here, are broken on the way. Minerals should be separately wrapped in paper or cloth before being put into the box. Eggs may safely be sent in augur holes bored in little blocks of wood. Flowers and ferns should be carefully pressed between strong sides of paste-board. Insects should be pinned with the utmost possible strength and care, into boxes thoroughly lined with cork, very strong, light, and doubly wrapped. Beetles and bugs may be sent in cotton, like eggs. Always prepay postage in full. Enclose no writing in the package (except the labels of the specimens; which are allowed) but never neglect to accompany the pack-

4

age with a postal card or letter, describing contents, stating from whom it comes, and rehearsing what you expect to receive in exchange. It is often utterly impossible to determine the sender of a package, or to know what to send in return. Tie the parcel strongly, but do not seal it, unless you wish to pay letter postage. One or two fine specimens are always more acceptable than several inferior ones. No propositions for exchange can be noticed in the *St. Nicholas*, excepting from members of the "A. A." For this, among other reasons, it is necessary for us to keep a full register of all members, and names of new members should always be sent us at once.

Finally, we cannot consider propositions to exchange coins, stamps, autographs, or any other articles, excepting such as properly come under the head of natural objects, or such as have scientific value. Whenever you send specimens as a voluntary contribution to the Lenox A. A. Cabinet, kindly state that you require no specimens in exchange. Your name shall be attached to the specimens when they are placed upon our shelves.

When you write to a sister chapter proposing an exchange, courtesy requires you to enclose a stamp for reply. Requests of this nature should always be promptly answered. Aim to give rather more than you receive. A grasping spirit of trade is utterly foreign to the nature of a true scientist.

CHAPTER XII.

THE BADGE.

No. 1.

The badge of the A. A. is a Swiss cross, of gold or silver. It is doubly appropriate, because Prof. Louis Agassiz was born in Switzerland, and because we took the hint for our organization from somewhat similar School Scientific Societies in that country. The number on the badge changes with each chapter, and is the number by which each chapter is known in the general organization. We are fortunate in having secured the services and interest of one of the most widely known badge, medal, and jewel manufacturers in the U. S., Mr. W. A. Hayward, 202 Broadway, N. Y. Badges can be obtained directly from him of either style here figured, at the following very low prices :

No. 1, or 2, solid silver, engraved, $ .50
No. 1, solid gold, engraved,   2.00
No. 1, solid gold, enameled,   3.00
No. 2, solid gold, engraved,   3.00
No. 2, solid gold, enameled,   4.00

No. 2.

We specially recommend size No. 1, in enameled gold. If the chapters wish anything else in Mr. Hayward's line, he will send an illustrated design by return mail.

CHAPTER XIII.

REPORTS FROM CHAPTERS AND CORRESPONDING MEMBERS.

Perhaps the actual working of our Society cannot better be illustrated than by giving a few extracts from the thousands of letters that constantly come to us from our friends of the A. A. We shall select such as contain practical suggestions for work ; and the first shows what may be done in the way of out-door excursions :

SALT LAKE CITY, UTAH.

I write to inform you of the organization of a Chapter of the Agassiz Association in Salt Lake City. Several of us boys have been more or less interested in natural history for some time, and when we read about the A. A. in *St. Nicholas*, we thought that it was just what we wanted. So on Wednesday, August 2d, four of us met and organized the Chapter.

We have already taken several tramps after specimens. On the first one we found the terminal moraine of a glacier, and our honorary member gave us a long description of glaciers—the manner of their formation and movements, and the way in which moraines are formed. Our last trip was to a mining district situated 9300 feet above the sea. It lasted five days, and we walked sixty miles, and found many rare Alpine plants, fossils, minerals, and bugs.

FRED. E. LEONARD, Box 265.

The next shows how Boards of Education help us :

HYDE PARK, ILLINOIS.

I am happy to inform you that a Natural History Association has been formed in our high school. We have 17 members, all of whom are very enthusiastic in their work. We all desire to connect ourselves with the A. A. We had a cabinet made, which cost $25.00. The Board of Education has kindly advanced the cost of this, provided we leave our collection in the building. They also allow us to meet in the building. We have an entrance fee of 50c., in order that none but "workers" may join. We are very careful about electing new members. Address

W. R. GWYNN, Box 237.

Among our most delightful branches, are what we call "Family Chapters," in which the members of one family unite to form a little society and study together.

FLUSHING, L. I.

I want to tell you how much we enjoy our meetings. The subject of the last meeting was Mistletoe, and here is what was said about it. Mamma said, "The botanical name of the mistletoe is *Viscum album*. In olden times it was thought to be poisonous, for Shakespeare speaks of the ' baleful Mistletoe.' The Druids used it in religious rites. It is a parasite, growing chiefly on apple-trees." Miss Scott had tasted the berry, which is sweet and glutinous. She painted me a lovely picture of mistletoe and holly. In the evenings when Papa is at home, we have music, and, if possible, pieces bearing on our subject; for instance, this evening we had a song entitled "The Mistletoe Bough." and an instrumental piece, the "Mistletoe Polka." Mamma plays on the violin, and I on the organ or piano.

From your friend, F. M. H.

There is no limit with regard to age. Little children have bright eyes.

THE OAKS, TIOGA CENTER, N. Y.

I am nine, and my sister is five. We have examined a geranium-bug, and it is beautiful. Its body is green, and it has six legs that are clear like crystal. The antennæ are longer than the insect, and are sometimes thrown backward. It has a long beak. The body has two horns at the end. The eyes are reddish brown, with tiny white dots.

ANGIE LATIMER, Sec.

St. Paul, Minn., Sept. 9, 1882.

Dear Mr. Ballard: We had a few caterpillars, but they all took off their hair, and lay down in it and died.

Frank Ramaley.

Several of our Chapters publish local papers.

Macomb, Ill.

Progressing nicely   We meet at each other's houses every Friday afternoon after school.   Almost all of us have been collecting insects during the summer.   We have a paper read every two weeks, to which we contribute original articles on anything pertaining to Natural History. The chapter is divided into two parts, and each part edits the paper alternately.   We cannot understand how other chapters have so nice club-rooms and cabinets and microscopes, etc.   Where do they get their money?   We like the A. A. *very much*.   Nellie H. Tunnicliff.

The next letter shows how to raise money when it is needed.

Buffalo, N. Y.

Our report is somewhat tardy, owing to an entertainment given for our microscope fund.   We realized $85, which, with the amount on hand, gives us about $100 to invest in a good instrument.   Our Chapter has increased to twenty-four active and two honorary members.   Owing to the lateness of the season, we have collectively made but one excursion, though individually we have not been idle.

Cora Freeman, Cor. Sec. B. Chapter A. A.

The girls are as enthusiastic workers as the boys.

We are pupils of the Waco Female College, Texas. About four years ago our teacher began to teach us to love nature, and, to keep our eyes and ears open, often took us to the woods.   Oh, how we enjoyed those rambles!   Such rides to and from the woods!   We soon got a collection, and determined to form a Natural History Society.   We were deliberating on a name when, to our great joy, your first article in *St. Nicholas* was read to us.   With a few variations we forthwith adopted the name, constitution, and by-laws. Since then we have varied with wind and weather, but have now launched upon a smooth-sailing sea. We have twenty-six members. Some of our prominent citizens have joined us. By carefully hoarding our dues of admission, etc., we have been able to buy a fine micro-scope, a number of shells, and a few books and pictures. We have a book in which the librarian pastes articles and pictures selected by some one member every week. We have another into which the Secretary transcribes the papers read by the members before the Society, and also articles of interest which can not be cut from valuable books. The President always appoints one member to ask three ques-tions to be answered at the next meeting. The correct answers are copied into our manuscript scrap-book. We often take questions from the *St. Nicholas.* Oh! we have so much to say to you, and to ask, I hardly know where to begin or leave off. We have a specimen of the Texas centi-pede for exchange, also a stinging lizard and a horned frog.

Miss JENNIE WISE, Box 554, Waco, Texas.

And our ranks are recruited by an increasing number of adult members, who are particularly welcome.

LAKE CITY, MINN., Oct. 19, 1882.
MR. H. H. BALLARD,

DEAR SIR: I have been deeply interested in your A. A. for some time back. and shall gladly become one of you in earnest. Such a union can not but result in the greatest benefit to our young people, opening, as it does, Nature's book to many of them with its inexhaustible pages, and the release from care in after years that their perusal will give.

If I remain here throughout the winter, I shall endeavor to bring some of our young folks together as a nucleus for a new Chapter. I can start them, at all events.

E. A. PATTON, M. D.

When a wide-awake teacher takes hold of the matter, the most important results follow.

About six months ago, Chapter 266, A. A., was organ-ized in connection with my school. We have succeeded wonderfully, both in point of numbers and collections. We now number thirty-three, and the prospects are that we shall soon have as many more. The boys, some twenty or more, have over five hundred specimens, consisting of fossils and insects. The girls, of whom we have lately added a dozen, are busily engaged in gathering leaves, roots, and seeds, and, when they make a report, we will classifiy them botanically. The whole neighborhood has been awakened by the enthusiasm of the boys and girls. All this work is collateral; that is, no part of school time is taken up. The County Superintendent of Schools was so delighted with the idea, that he has earnestly requested me to bring the matter before our County Institute, the third week in December. The Institute numbers six hundred teachers, and if this is done, the A. A., no doubt, will spread in this county.   T. G. JONES, St. Clair, Schuyl. Co., Pa.

Another marked instance is that of Chapter 285, Greenfield, Mass., as shown by this extract from the _Springfield Republican_ :

"Principal Sanderson started a good deal of zeal among the high school pupils, some two years ago, in the study of natural history, and as a result the natural history society was organized. The work began in a small way in the collection of birds, plants, and minerals, until the foundation has been laid for a permanent museum. The Society now has one large case of stuffed birds, containing 150 well-preserved specimens. These are mostly native birds, caught and mounted by members of the Society. Several in this way have become quite expert taxidermists. The Society belongs to the Agassiz Association, and by exchanges has added to some of the departments. The local organization is made up of thirty-six members, who were ambitious enough, last fall, to hire of the town the old brick house near the high-school building, paying a rental of $150 a year. These youthful scientific investigators want encouragement from the citizens at large, and are going to ask the town, at its annual meeting, to contribute the rent of this building. It would seem that the voters could very properly encourage the young people in this way. As the natural history rooms are located close to the high-school building, it can very readily be made a beneficial adjunct to the public schools. Already the zoological classes have enjoyed the advantages of these rooms and their collections."

A love for Nature often affects the whole character.

But the best of all, and that for which I want sincerely to thank the "A. A." and its projector, is the result of the work in one particular case. As a teacher, you know how difficult it is to do just the best thing with a roguish, careless boy, smart, but caring little for study and with little or no will to work. Geology last year and chemistry this, prepared him for an elementary course in determinative mineralogy. This he has undertaken, under the guise of association work, and to this we largely attribute a most wonderful improvement in the boy. Spare moments are spent in the laboratory instead of in mischief; he has begged to return to Latin, which he had dropped, and bids fair to stand at or near the head of his class in that and other studies. Instead of lawless lounging at recess, he is quiet and gentlemanly.　　　　　A Friend.

Boys can accomplish excellent results by themselves.

Another eventful year has passed, and left "success" written on all our records. During the year, 31 essays have been read, and 21 regularly announced discussions have been successfully held. Our roll of members has been increased from 13 to 18. In our library are 68 bound volumes, and 439 magazines. Besides these, we have a scrap-book, folio, and several charts, and files of essays. We have a balance of $64.83 to our credit.
　　　　　A. Nehrbas, Sec., New York, B.

Many chapters study animals alive.

　　　　　Racine, Wis.
A.—We intend to begin collecting plants as soon as the snow is off the ground. We shall also make a collection of the skeletons of the fish we catch next year. We have a place arranged for an aviary, also. We had an aquarium running all last year.　　　　　John L. McCalman, Sec.

Valuable libraries and reading rooms are founded in connection with the A. A.

MONTREAL, CANADA.

We have a splendid cabinet, 6 feet high, 3 feet wide, and 2 feet deep, containing forty-eight drawers, twenty-two of which are allotted to the entomological section. Nineteen of these are already filled with insects. Our library promises to become a great success. We are trying to secure a room in the St. Antoine School for a museum and reading room. We have had two very successful field-meetings, on one of which prizes were offered for the best collection made during the day. I expect to see the Montreal branch of the A. A. take a leading position among the scientific institutions of Canada. One of our most successful evenings was spent with the microscope. W. D. SHAW.

In some cases, members take turns in giving lectures.

We have given a parlor concert. C. K. Liuson gave us a "chalk talk." At one side of the parlor we had a table with some specimens on it; and after the entertainment we invited our friends to inspect them. We have now money enough to get a cabinet. We have decided to have a course of lectures—one delivered by each member on his chosen branch. A. D. PHILLIPS, Brooklyn, E.

I append a few

NOTES

that have been made by members of the A. A., partly to show what sort of work is being done, and partly to furnish a suggestion to new members of what they can do. These notes, as well as the letters from chapters and friends already given, are taken almost at random from our monthly reports that have appeared in *St. Nicholas.* Those wishing a full knowledge of our work, must refer to the . numbers of that magazine since November, 1880.

I have observed with great interest the rise and progress of the A. A., and write this note to contribute a suggestion for their use. One of the most desirable modes of
research would be to raise wild plants from seed, for the
purpose of ascertaining the limits of variation in certain
groups. Especially interesting for this inquiry are the
Canadensis section of *Solidago*, *Vaccinium Pennsylvanicum*,
Aster corymbosus and *lævis*, and *Datura Stramonium*. Let
each person collect the seeds of a single plant only, which
should be carefully identified, and sow and cultivate them
till maturity.   WM II. SEAMAN,
                          Prof. Chem., Washington, D. C.

Silk worms—What they will eat.—Not being able to
obtain white mulberry leaves, which are, I believe, the
only mulberry leaves on which the *Bombyx mori* will thrive,
I fed them on leaves of Osage-orange. At the time I was
raising about 2000 larvæ. These leaves must be plucked
sometime before, so as to allow them to wilt before giving
them to the worms. This rule must be rigidly observed. I
made an experiment to test it. I placed four healthy worms
in a sieve by themselves, and fed them exclusively on fresh
leaves. They grew wonderfully, and reached their largest
size before the others; but as soon as they began to spin
they grew sickly and weak, and after forming slight
cocoons, died entangled in the silk. Most of those fed on
wilted leaves spun well. If the question were simply,
"What will silk-worms *eat?*" I might answer, with a good
degree of accuracy, that they will eat every leaf that grows;
but as I know you desire to know what they will *thrive* on,
I highly recommend Osage-orange.—A Friend of the A. A.

Flowers under a handkerchief.—We came to a spot
which Dr. Hammond covered with his handkerchief, and
we guessed how many kinds of plants were growing under
it. There were ten: a violet, a dandelion, an aster, a
buttercup, a hepatica, a fern, a Mitchella vine, a daisy, a
plantain, a veronica.—Emily S. Warren.

Winter.—I feel as keen delight in the approach of
winter as I should if spring, with all her glories, were at the
gate. For me, the vast white carpet, absolutely without
a stain, the low-hanging sun, and the trees that respond to

the winter wind, have peculiar charms.—Linwood M.
Howe, Hallowell, Me.

Cow Black bird.—I found four cow-birds' eggs in a nest
with one egg of the Wilson's thrush. Has any one else
found so many in one nest?—X.

Night-hawk asleep.—Last August, I saw, about seven
o'clock one evening. what I took to be a dead bird lying on
a stone wall by the road-side. It was half lying, half lean-
ing, against a stone. I clambered up the bank to get it,
making some noise. Just as I put out my hand to pick it
up, with a great flap and rush by my face, the bird soared
up into the air. As soon as it opened its wings, I knew it
to be a night-hawk by the white spots on the under side of
them, and by the peculiar cry it uttered.—Wm. Carter.

Humming-birds learn by experience.—A young lady
watched some humming-birds taking nectar from the
flowers of our abutilon. The full-grown birds pushed their
bills in between the calyx and corolla, just as the bees I
wrote of some months ago, nipped a hole in the petunias, in
order to get more easily at the nectar. But the most curious
thing is, that the young birds tried to take their drink in
the ordinary way. by going inside the bell of the flower,
and it was only as they grew in wisdom and stature that
they learned from their parents the shorter way. The
young lady is quite confident that the smaller birds were
not of a different kind, but the young of the larger
birds.—C.

We have received the heartiest sympathy and
help from a large number of distinguished and

GENEROUS SCIENTISTS.

I shall present later a classified list of these gentlemen, but I cannot forbear giving here a few of their
kind letters, to illustrate the utterly unselfish and
philanthropic spirit that animates men thoroughly
devoted to Natural Science.

" I have watched, with more interest than I can readily
communicate, the genesis and development of the A. A. In

answer to your call for assistance, I shall be most happy to identify minerals and the commoner forms of paleozoic fossils. WM. M. BOWRON. [F. C. S.]
South Pittsburg, Tenn."

"DEPARTMENT OF AGRICULTURE,
"DIVISION OF ENTOMOLOGY, WASHINGTON, D. C.

"I chanced to pick up a number of *St. Nicholas* this evening, and learned for the first time of the A. A., and saw evidences of its good work. I also noticed your call for an entomologist, and desire to offer my services. Our facilities here for identifying species in the great group of insects are exceptionally good, and I should be very glad if I could help any boy or girl in his or her studies in that direction. LELAND O. HOWARD."

"CORNELL UNIV., ITHACA, N. Y., Jan. 20, 1883.

"I have not yet outgrown my sympathy for the younger people. I will gladly answer their questions so far as time will permit, and will *make* time for their sakes, even when I am busy. My especial department is certain parts of Phænogamic and Cryptogamic Botany; among other things, the *grasses, ferns,* and *mosses.*
"I shall always be delighted to serve the boys and girls, even at the busiest moments. WILLIAM RUSSELL DUDLEY."

WATERVILLE, MAINE, March 20, 1883.
"I read with much interest the account of the Agassiz Association in last *St. Nicholas.* It is a work that has my heartiest sympathy, and I would like it to have also what little cooperation I may be able to render. I shall be happy to answer questions relating to the mineralogy of Maine. CHAS. B. WILSON,
"Instructor Nat. Sc., Colby University."

" If your correspondents desire the names of any ferns, grasses, or plants in general, or any information on the subject of botany, I shall be glad to answer all such, or at least all that come from west of the Mississippi. I realize the value of such work as you are doing.
"MARCUS E. JONES, Salt Lake City, Utah.

"ACADEMY NATURAL SCIENCE, OF PHILADELPHIA,
"19th and Race streets, March 1, 1883.

"Having seen your call in *St. Nicholas* of this month, for assistance in answering the many questions brought forward by the members of the A. A., I take pleasure in offering my aid. My specialties are entomology and conchology. With earnest desire for the success of the society,

G. HOWARD PARKER.

"MILWAUKEE, WIS., March 30, 1884.

"I am working on the Jumping Spiders (*Attidæ*), of the world. I should be very happy to determine spiders in this group from any locality, for members of the A. A.

GEO. W. PECKHAM."

"I should be glad to assist the A. A. in any matter relating to marine zoology. C. F. HOLDER,

Am. Museum Nat. Hist.,
Central Park (77th St. and 8th Ave.), N. Y.

———

These gentlemen and the others who have thus freely offered their aid can hardly realize how great a service they are rendering. Here are over 7000 young and older amateur naturalists belonging to our society, most of whom, living in remote towns, have few opportunities of instruction in the subjects of their choice. They are now placed in such a position that they can go on with their observations without leaving home ; can be advised as to the best books for consultation in their several departments ; can exchange specimens and thoughts with members in all the different States and Territories ; and can have the assistance of men trained in special departments of science, and all without expense. May not the A. A. be the means of solving one of the most perplexing educational questions of the day ?

CHAPTER XIV.

ADDRESSES OF SPECIALISTS.

The names and addresses of the gentlemen that
have volunteered to aid us by answering questions
in their several departments, are here given, and any
member of the A. A. is at liberty to consult them
regarding whatever perplexity he may meet in his
branch of study, special heed being paid to the conditions of correspondence added below.

BOTANY.

I. N. E. States and Canada............Prof. C. H. K. Sanderson,
Greenfield, Mass.
II. Middle States......................Dr. Charles Atwood,
Moravia, N. Y.
III. Middle States......................Prof. W. R. Dudley,
(Ferns, sedges and grasses), Ithaca, N. Y.
IV. Middle States......................Prof. Edw. L. French,
Wells College, Aurora, N. Y.
V. Southern States.................Dr. Chapman,
Apalachicola, Fla.
VI. Western States to Colorado.........Dr. Aug. F. Foerste,
(Puff-balls a specialty), Dayton, O.
VII. Far West and North-west. ....Dr. Marcus E. Jones,
Salt Lake City, Utah.
VIII. In General..............   ....Prof. W. Trealease, S. B.,
Univ. Wis., Madison, Wis.

CONCHOLOGY.

I. Prof. Bruce Richards, 1726 N. 18th st., Philadelphia, Pa.
II. Mr. Thomas Morgan, Somerville, N. J.
III. Mr. H. A. Pilsbry, Davenport, Iowa.
IV. Prof. C. Howard Parker, 688 Main st., Cambridge, Mass.
V. Mr. Harry E. Dore, 521 Clay st., San Francisco, Cal. (*Pacific Mollusca*).

ENTOMOLOGY.

I. Prof. G. Howard Parker (address above).
II. Prof. C. H. Fernald, State College, Orono, Me. (*Lepidoptera*).
III. Mr. H. L. Fernald, Orono, Me. (*Hemiptera*).
IV. Prof. Leland O. Howard, Dep. Agriculture, Entomological
Div., Washington, D. C.

V. Prof. H. Atwood, Office Germania Life Ins. Co., Rochester, N. Y. (*Parasites and microscopic infusoria*).
VI. Dr. Aug. F. Foerste, Dayton, O. (*Spiders*).
VII. Mr. Fred C. Bowditch, Tappan st., Brookline, Mass. (*Coleoptera*).
VIII. Mr. A. W. Putman-Cramer, 51 Douglass st., Brooklyn, N. Y. (*Macro-Lepidoptera*).
IX. Prof. J. A. Lintner (State Entomologist), New Capitol, Albany, N. Y.

Ethnology.

I. Prof. H. T. Cresson, Acad. Nat. Sc., cor. 19th and Race sts., Philadelphia, Pa.

Geology.

I. Mr. Wm. H. Briggs, Columbia, Cal.
II. Mr. Jas. C. Lathrop, 134 Park ave., Bridgeport, Conn.
III. Mr. W. R. Lighton, Ottumwa, Iowa.
IV. Prof. Wm. M. Bowron, South Pittsburg. Tenn.
V. Prof. C. R. Vanhise, M. S., Univ. Wis., Madison, Wis.

Mineralogy.

I. Prof. Wm. R. Bowron (address above).
II. Mr. Jas. C. Lathrop (address above).
III. Prof. F. W. Staebner, Westfield, Mass.
IV. Mr. Chas. B. Wilson, Colby University, Waterville, Me. (*Minerals of Maine*).
V. Mr. David Allan, box 113, Webster Groves, Missouri.
VI. Prof. S. F. Peckham, Bristol, R. I.

Oology.

I. D. H. Eaton, Woburn, Mass., Box 1235.
II. F. H. Lattin, Gaines, N. Y.

Ornithology.

I. Mr. James De B. Abbott, Germantown, Pa.
II. Mr. Arthur P. Chadbourne, 21 Buckingham st., Cambridge, Mass.
III. Prof. S. W. Willard (*Wisconsin Birds*), West De Pere, Wis.
IV. Prof. C. A. Menefee, Los Gatos, California.

Physiology.

I. Chas. Everett Warren, M. D., 51 Union Park, Boston, Mass.
II. Wm. M. Baird, M. D., Washington, N. J.

Zoology.

I. Dr. C. F. Holder, American Museum Nat. Hist., Central Park N. Y., 77th st. and Eighth ave. (*Marine Life*).
II. Dr. Aug. Foerste, Dayton, O. (*Mammals*).
III. Prof. E. A. Birge, Ph.D., Univ. Wis., Madison, Wis.

CONDITIONS OF CORRESPONDENCE.

The following rules must be strictly regarded not only in corresponding with the gentlemen just named, but also in addressing the President.

1st. *Enclose in each letter requiring an answer, a stamped and self-addressed envelope, or a postal card. (The envelope is better, as we frequently wish to reply by a circular, or full letter.)*

2d. *Do not write for assistance until you have tried your best to succeed without it. That is : Do not ask lazy questions. Consult the index of this book and see if the answer cannot be found within.*

3d. *Use the ordinary size and style of writing paper, and write only on one side of the leaf.*

4th. *Give your full address in each letter, and give P. O. Box rather than street and number. State also the number of the Chapter of which you are a member.*

5th. *Do not waste time by sending letters or notices of exchange to the St. Nicholas. It merely causes the editors the trouble of re-mailing them to the President.*

CHAPTER XV.

BOOKS RECOMMENDED.

(The Roman numerals refer to the Publishers' addresses given below. Books marked * are Illustrated.)

BIOLOGY.

Huxley, T. H.   Physical Basis of Life.   15c.   I.
Magginley, T. C.   *Biology. $1.25.   1I.
Stevenson, S. H.   *Boys and Girls in Biology. $150.   III.
Wythe, J. H.   Easy Lessons in Vegetable
 Biology.   40c.   XXIV.

BOTANY.

Bailey, W. W. *Collector's Hand-book.   (Very
 valuable.) $1.50.   XXX.
Bessey, C. E.   Botany. (One of the latest and best.) VIII.
Brown, D. T.   *Trees of America.   (Popular and
 Sc.) $5.50.   VI.
Darwin, Chas.   Insectivorous Plants. $2.00.   III.
 "   *Variations of Animals and
 Plants. $5.00.   III.
Goodale, G. L.   *A few Common Plants.   25c.   IX.
Gray, A.   *Manual of Botany, with Lessons. $3.00.   IV.
 "   *School and Field Botany. $2.50.   IV.
 "   *Structural and Systematic Botany. $3.50. IV.
Herrick S. B.   *Wonders of Plant Life. $1.50.   II.
Hervey, Rev. A. B.   *Sea Mosses.   A complete
 Guide. $2.00.   .   . XXX.
Hooker, Sir W. J.   *Every Known Fern. $11.00.   II.
Hough, F. B.   Elements of Forestry. $2.00.   V.
Jones, Marcus E.   Ferns of the West.   30c.   X.
Pendleton, E. M.   Scientific Agriculture, $1.50.   VII.
Underwood, L. M., Ph. D.   *Our Native Ferns.
 $1.50.   XXX.
Willis, O. R.   Flora of New Jersey. $1.00.   VII.
Wood, A.   *American Botanist and Florist. $2.50.   VII.
 "   *Class Book of Botany. $3.50.   VI1.
Wood, H. C. *Fresh Water Algæ of N. A. $7.50.   II.
Youmans, E, A.   *First Book of Botany.   85c.   III.

ENTOMOLOGY.

Ballard, J. P. *Insect Lives. $1.00. V.
Conant, II. S. *Butterfly Hunters. $1.50. XI.
Edwards. Butterflies of N. A. 1st series, $30.00.
   2d series, in parts, each $2.50. XII.
Harris, T. W. *Insects Injurious to Vegetation.
   $4.00 and $6.50. XIV.
Lubbock, Sir John. *Ants, Bees and Wasps. $2.00. III.
Manton. How to Catch Insects. 50c. XXII.
Packard, A. S. Jr. *Guide to Study of Insects.
   $5.00. VIII.
Richmond, G. II. Insect Collecting. 10c. XV.

GEOLOGY.

Agassiz, L. Sketches. 2 vols. Each $2.50. XII.
Crosby, W. Common Minerals and Rocks. 35c.
   (With 50 labeled specimens, $1.50.) IX.
Dana, J. D. *Manual of Geology. $5.00. IV.
" Geological Story, briefly told. $1.50. IV.
Geikie, A. Geology. 50c. III.
Hovey, H. C. *Celebrated American Caverns. $2.00. V.
Huxley, T. II. Geology. 50c. III.
Kingsley, Chas. Town Geology. 15c. I.
Mantell, G. A. Petrifactions and their Teachings.
   $2.50. XVIII.
Shaler, N. S. *Fossil Branchiopods of the Ohio.
   $2.50. V.
Tyndall, J. *Forms of Water. 15c. I.
Winchell, Alex. *World Life. $2.50. XVII.
" " `Sparks from a Geologist's
   Hammer. $2.00. XVII.
Winchell, Alex. *Geological Excursions (for
   young learners). XVII.

MICROSCOPY.

Davies, T. *Preparation of Objects. $1.50. II.
Gosse, P. H. *Evenings at the Microscope. $1.50. III.
Phin, J. *Practical Hints on Selection and use of
   a Microscope. 75c. (abridged 30c.), XIX.
Wood, J. G. Common Objects. 400 illustra-
   tions. 50c. XIX.

MINERALOGY.

Brush, G. J. *Manual of Determinative Mineralogy
     and Blow-pipe Analysis. $3.00.   XX.
Dana, J. D. Manual of Minerology. $1.50.   XXXII.
Hyatt, A. Pebbles. 35c.   XI.

NATURAL HISTORY.

Agassiz, Mrs. *First Lesson in Nat. Hist. 30c.   IX.,
Agassiz, L. Methods of Study. $1.50.   XI.
Albertsen, F. *Four-footed Lovers. (For children).
    $1.00.   XXII.
Chadbourne, P. A. Lectures. 75c.   VII.
Cecil's *Natural History. 85c.   XXI.
Darwin, C. Vegetable Mould and Earthworms.
    $1.50.   III.
Harris, A. B. *Door Yard Folks. $1.00.   XXIII.
Hinton, J. *Life in Nature. 15c.   I.
Hooker, W. *Child's Book of Nature. 3 parts.
    No. 1, 60c.; 2 and 3, each 65c.; bound
    in one, $1.60.   VI.
Huxley, T. H. *Physiography. An introduction
    to the study of Nature. (Very valuable.)
    $2.50.   III.
Ingersoll, Ernest. *Old Ocean $1.00.   XXIII.
Kingsley. *Naturalists' Assistant. A complete
    guide to the care of the cabinet.   XXXI.
Johonnot, J. *A Natural History Reader. $1.25.   III.
White, G. Selborne. 75c.   VI.

ORNITHOLOGY.

Austin. *Taxidermy without a Teacher. 50c.   XXII.
Baird, S. F. *Land Birds of California. $10.00.   XXV.
Brown, T. *Manual of Taxidermy. $1.50.   II.
Coues, Elliott. *Birds of the Northwest. $4.50.   XXX1.
Coues, Elliott. *Key to North American Birds,
    including " Field Ornithology." $10.00.   XXVI.
Jasper, T. Birds of N. A. Col. plates, in 40
    parts at $1.00 each, or 2 vols.; royal 4to.
    Half morocco, $50; full morocco, $60.   V:

Minot, H. D. *Land and Game Birds of N. E.
The birds, their nests, eggs, habits and
notes. 1 vol. [An excellent book.]   XXVI.
Stearns, W. A. *Bird Life; a Manual of Orni-
thology. $5.00.   XXII.
Willard, S. L. *Manual of Oology. $1.50.   XIII.

ZOOLOGY.

Buckland, F. T. *Log-book of Zoologist. $3.00.   XVIII.
Buckley, A. B. *Life and her Children. $1.50.   III.
" *Winners in Life's Race. $1.50.   III.
Butler, H. D. Family Aquarium. 75c.   I.
Check-list of North American Shells. 25c.   XXVII.
Darwin, Chas. Origin of Species. $2.00.   III.
" *Descent of Man. $3.00.   III.
Emerton, J. H. Structure and Habits of Spiders.
$1.50.   XIII.
Garman, Samuel. *Reptiles and Batrachians of N.
A. 4to. pp. 185, 9 pl. paper. $4.00.   V.
Girard, C. *Fresh Water Fish of N. A. $1.50.   XXVII.
Gosse, P. H. *Romance of Nat. Hist.   XVIII.
Huxley, T. H. *The Crayfish. An introduction
to the study of Zoology. 82m. $1 75.   III.
Huxley, T. H. Origin of Species. 15c.   I.
" Lectures on Evolution. 15c.   I.
Hyatt, A. *Oyster, Clam, etc. 30c.   IX.
" *Hydroids, Corals, etc. 25c.   IX.
" *Sponges. 25c.   IX.
Mivart. The Cat. [For advanced students.]   XVI.
Morse, E. S. *First book of Zoology.   III.
Mulertt, Hugo. *The Goldfish and its Culture.
$1.00.   V.
Steele, J. D. *14 weeks in Zoology. $1.50.   VII.
Tenney, S. *Manual of Zoology. $3 and $4   XXVIII.
Wilson, Andrew, Ph. D. Facts and Fictions of
Z. 15c.   I.
Wood, J. G. *Homes without Hands. $4.50.   VI.
Woodward. Manual of Mollusca.   XXVII.

MISCELLANEOUS.

Agassiz, L. *Journey in Brazil. $3.00.   XII.
Brightwell, C. L. Lives of Labor. $1.25.

Gatty, Mrs. A.   *Parables from Nature. 75c.   XXIX.
Huxley. T. H.   Darwin and Humboldt. 15c.   I.
Ingersoll, Ernest.   *Friends worth Knowing. $1.   VI.
Manton.   Hand-book for Water Drinkers. 50c.   XXII.
Mudie, R.   Observations of Nature. 75c.   VI.
Smiles, Samuel.   *Scotch Naturalist. $1.50.   VI.
  "   *Robert Dick; Baker, Geologist
    and Botanist. $1.50.   V1.

The Naturalist's Directory: containing an alphabetical list
of nearly all the Naturalists of the U. S., with their
specialties and addresses.   XIII.

Herbarium—Ballard, H. H., and Thayer, S. P.   For the
convenient preservation of flowers, ferns and leaves.
$1 to $3.50.   Contains directions for collecting and
preserving plants; Blanks for an Analytical Record of
each specimen, pages for mounting plants, and gummed
paper to fasten them. 20 per cent. discount to members of
the A. A.   Address the Author.

PUBLISHERS' ADDRESSES.

I.   J. Fitzgerald, 20 Lafayette place, N. Y.
II.   G. P. Putnam's Sons, 27 W. 23d street, N. Y.
III.   D. Appleton & Co., 1 Bond street. N. Y.
IV.   Ivison, Blakeman, Taylor & Co., 138 Grand
      street, New York.
V.   Robert Clarke & Co., 61 W. 4th street,
      Cincinnati, Ohio.
VI.   Harper & Brothers, Franklin Square, N. Y.
VII.   A. S. Barnes & Co., 1 William st., N. Y.
VIII.   Henry Holt & Co., 29 W. 23d st., N. Y.
IX.   Ginn & Heath, 9 Tremont Pl., Boston. Mass.
X.   Dr. Marcus E. Jones, Salt Lake City, Utah.
XI.   James R. Osgood & Co., 211 Tremont street,
      Boston, Mass.
XII.   Houghton, Mifflin & Co., 4 Park street,
      Boston, Mass.
XIII.   S. E. Cassino & Co., 41 Arch st., Boston, Mass.
XIV.   Orange Judd Company, 245 Broadway, N. Y.
XV.   G. H. Richmond, Northfield, Vt.

XVI. MacMillan & Co., 112 4th ave.. N. Y.
XVII. S. C. Griggs & Co., 87 Wabash ave., Chicago, Ill.
XVIII. J. B. Lippincott & Co., 715 Market street, Philadelphia, Pa.
XIX. Industrial Publication Co., 176 Broadway, N. Y.
XX. John Wiley, 15 Astor place, New York city.
XXI. John B. Alden, 393 Pearl street, N. Y.
XXII. Lee & Shepard, 47 Franklin st., Boston. Mass.
XXIII. D. Lothrop & Co., 32 Franklin st., Boston. Mass.
XXIV. Phillips & Hunt (headquarters of C. L. S. C., Pubs.), 805 Broadway, New York.
XXV. Little, Brown & Co., 254 Washington street, Boston, Mass.
XXVI. Estes & Lauriat, 303 Washington street, Boston, Mass.
XXVII. Smithsonian Institute, Washington, D. C.
XXVIII. Scribner & Welford, 745 Broadway, New York.
XXIX. Th. Nelson & Son, 42 Bleecker st., N. Y.
XXX. E. A. Bates, Salem, Mass.
XXXI. Frank H. Lattin, Gaines, Orleans Co., N. Y.
XXXII. Henry W. Peck, New Haven, Ct.

NOTES.

As some may be bewildered by the great number of books here named, we will mention a few that seem to us especially adapted to the wants of the majority of the members of the A. A.

In Botany, if we could have only one book, we would take Gray's Manual and Lessons; but Prof. Wood gives fuller descriptions, and his " Class-book of Botany "works in" very conveniently with Gray's. Both these books lead rapidly to analysis and classification.

Youman's Lessons and Bessey's Botany lead rather to personal observation, and to a plan of study more in accord with modern methods in Biology.

" Wonders of Plant Life" shows many of the beauties revealed by the microscope, and is fully illustrated.

In Entomology, we recommend for the first choice, " Harris, on Insects injurious to Vegetation," as we know of no better general work on insects; Packard's Guide, perhaps, comes next, and in some respects, such as anatomical detail, is much fuller. It is not quite so simple for the tyro.

Insect Lives, gives the life history of many of our common Lepidoptera, with hints on the rearing of larvæ, etc., and has proved wonderfully stimulating to many of the A. A. It is published by Robert Clarke of Cincinnati, who has just completed the publication of Jasper's magnificent work on the Birds of North America.

Lubbock's book on Ants, is a fascinating record of the observations and experiments of that distinguished naturalist.

In Geology, Dana's are the standard text-books. Nothing can be better for beginners, however, than Common Minerals and Rocks, with the accompanying set of specimens. It is wonderfully cheap.

Every one should read at least one of Huxley's books, and with whichever he begins, he is pretty sure to get the others afterward.

Chas. Kingsley's "Town Geology" is popular and valuable, and as it can be gotten for 15 cents, being one of the famous " Humboldt Library," which has done so much to make science popular in America, there is no reason why every one should not buy it, as an experiment if nothing more. The same is doubly true of Tyndall's " Forms of Water."

Prof. Winchell's three books, from the elegant press of Griggs & Co., do not aim at systematic teaching; they are not text-books; but they are thoroughly interesting and instructive. " Geological Excursion is charming, and we confidently recommend them all for every Naturalist's library.

In Natural History, there is nothing for the price, to compare with "Cecil's." For the little folks, Four-footed Lovers; Door-yard Folks; Old Ocean, are excellent, while for those a little older we recommend Hooker.

Darwin's book on Worms, is even more valuable as illustrating the accurate and patent methods of work that made its author the greatest Naturalist of his age, than for the wonderful facts it narrates.

If only one book, however, can be chosen from the list, and you are too old for Hooker, try Huxley. You will read 'Selborne' as a matter of course.

In Ornithology, price must guide you. The books are all excellent.

In Zoology, for a general manual, get Tenney; for pleasant reading, Wood; for guide to methods of scientific work, Mivart, Huxley, or Hyatt. The special works speak for themselves.

Among the miscellaneous books, you would derive most pleasure and lasting benefit from " Parables from Nature." Mr. Smiles' books illustrate his favorite subject, 'Self-help,' and show how much young people can accomplish alone, if they *will*.

It will be noted that Appleton & Co. publish books whose prices average about $2 or $3. They are beautifully printed and bound, and it pays to get them.

Ginn & Heath have done the public a great service by their elegant series of cheap books. These are cheap only in price, for they are thoroughly well printed, on excellent paper, and richly illustrated.

They are small, and in heavy paper covers. You can well afford the entire series.

Fitzgerald & Co. bring the choicest works of the greatest thinkers of Europe, within reach of the poorest boy among us. Every chapter of the A. A. should get the catalogue of the Humboldt Library, and keep it for reference. We advise you to buy finely bound books, it you can afford it, but if you cannot, you will rejoice at this opportunity of getting them in paper.

If any of you wish to take regular courses of study together, you will do well to write to A. S. Barnes & Co., and get some of Prof. Steele's " 14 weeks" series. This includes, besides the 'Zoology,' " 14 weeks in Geology, Physiology, Botany, Chemistry, Astronomy, and Physics."

Whenever you write to any of these firms for books, you should state that you are a member of the Agassiz Association.

Doubtless very many books have been omitted from our list that would have been included, had they been brought to our knowledge, and we shall esteem it a favor if our friends will, from time to time, send us the names, prices, and Publishers' addresses of such books as may seem to them specially worthy of recommendation.

MAGAZINES AND PAPERS.

The Auk, is a quarterly journal of Ornithology, published at \$3.00 a year by Estes & Lauriat, Boston, Mass. Mr. J. A. Allen and Dr. Elliot Coues, are on the editorial staff. Each number contains about 100 pages, and, occasionally, colored plates.

The American Naturalist, is a monthly devoted to the Natural Sciences in their widest sense. It is published by McCalla & Stavely, 257 Dock Street, Philadelphia, Pa., at $4. It is rather scientific than popular, but not so technical as to be 'hard reading,' and numbers among its contributors many of our most distinguished naturalists.

The Ornithologist and Oologist, is published monthly, at $1 per year, by Frank B. Webster, Pawtucket, R. I. It is well illustrated, wide awake, and not beyond the comprehension of our young bird-lovers and egg-hunters.

Science Record. S. E. Cassino & Co., 41 Arch Street, Boston, Mass., is a monthly journal of Notes and News in all departments of Science. It costs only a dollar a year, is illustrated, handsomely printed, and popular.

The Microscopical Bulletin, is a valuable little bimonthly paper, published at 25 cents a year, by James W. Queen & Co., 924 Chestnut Street, Philadelphia. [" Bi-monthly" means once in two months, not twice in one month.]

Science. Science Co., Cambridge, Mass. $5.00. Best adapted to the wants of professional Scientists, it contains also many articles of general interest, popularly written. It is a weekly illustrated magazine.

Nature. A weekly illustrated journal of Science. MacMillan & Co., Publishers, 112 4th Avenue, N. Y. This is an English journal, and corresponds in its leading features to "*Science.*" It is perhaps not quite so technical, and the price is $6 per annum. " Nature," " Science," and " The American Natu-

ralist," stand in the front rank of Scientific periodicals.

Popular Science News, is a $1 monthly, published
by the Popular Science News Co., at 19 Pearl-st.,
Boston, Mass. "The end and aim of 'Science
News,' is to furnish a cheap journal of reliable scientific information." It is illustrated, and good.
Dr. Nichol's new book, "Whence, What, Where?"
is given as a premium to each new subscriber.

Forest and Stream, published weekly at $4.00 a
year, " is the recognized medium of entertainment,
instruction, and information between American
Sportsmen." It is a very large paper, and among its
regular departments are "Natural History," "Sea
and River Fishing," "The Kennel," "Rifle Shooting," and "Canoeing." 39 Park Row, N. Y. City.

Bulletin of Massachusetts Natural History, is a
monthly journal edited and published at Amherst,
Mass., by Prof. W. A. Stearns, author of "Bird-
life," the popular manual of Ornithology. It is specially devoted to the Natural History of Massachusetts, but contains much of general interest. It
costs only $1 a year.

The Kansas City Review of Science and Industry.
" This is a strictly popular magazine, perhaps better
adapted to family reading than any other scientific
journal in the country." It comprises original articles by the best writers, and selections from the best
periodicals of this country and Europe, upon Geology, Mining, Archæology, Meteorology, Biography,
etc. Monthly, 64 pp. octavo, $2.50 per year. Clubs
of four or more allowed a discount of 25 per cent.
Theodore S. Case, Kansas City, Mo.

The Naturalist's Journal, a monthly, for 50 cents

a year, is published by Mr. R. T. Taylor, Frankford,
Pa. It is an admirable paper, and represents the local
interests of the A. A.

The Young Naturalist, a 50 cent monthly, is published by another of our enterprising members, in
Galesburgh, Ill. The Editor, Mr. C. F. Gettemy,
modestly disclaims attempting to represent the A. A.,
but his paper is, after all, a good representative of
the energy and enthusiasm of our Illinois Chapters.

The Amateur Naturalist, is published monthly,
for 30 cents a year, by still another of our young
friends, Mr. Elliston J. Perot, 5103 Main Street,
Germantown, Pa. It is an excellent paper, and has
our best wishes.

The Young Oologist, is published by Mr. Frank
H. Lattin, Gaines, Orleans Co., N. Y. It is a
bright paper, which gives in popular language, a
great amount of useful information about bird's-
eggs, nests, and collecting.

The Young Scientist, published at $1 per year, by
the Industrial Publishing Co., 294 Broadway, N. Y.,
contains among other things an exchange column,
and a column of notes and queries.

Random Notes is a bright little paper published
by Southwick & Jencks, Providence, R. I. See next
chapter.

St. Nicholas, *Union Square, N. Y.* $3 a year.
This is the leading Magazine for young people. It
is replete with stories by the best authors, and pictures by the best artists. It is the "Official Organ"
of the Agassiz Association.

CHAPTER XVI.

In response to often repeated inquiries, we present a directory of leading and reliable dealers in everything a Naturalist can need.   In ordering supplies, state that you are a member of the A. A.

All Naturalists' Supplies, including books and specimens, can be ordered of Prof. A. E. Foote, 1223 Belmont Ave., Philadelphia, Pa.   He has a large and valuable collection of Natural objects, accurately labeled.   Prof. Foote is very courteous, and treats young members of the A. A. as patiently and generously as men that send him thousand dollar orders.   Since our first edition, we have heard good words of Prof. F. from many members.   His set of 100 minerals for $1, is a wonder of excellence and cheapness.

Chemicals and Chemical Apparatus.   Many of our members are especially interested in Chemistry. They will be glad to know that Bullock & Crenshaw, 528 Arch Street, Philadelphia, are manufacturers and importers of both the chemicals and the apparatus, suitable for Analytical, Technical and Experimental use.   You can get a descriptive priced catalogue free on application.

Microscopes and Accessories.   Perhaps we have had more queries about microscopes than any other one thing.   As you can get a microscope at almost any price from 30 cents to $1650.00, you should send 10 cents to W. H. Walmsley & Co., 1016 Chestnut Street, Phila., and get their illustrated catalogue,

part first. Then with the advice of that firm, you
can select just what you want.

After you get your Microscope, you can find
nothing so good or so cheap to keep your slides in
as what is called " Pillsbury's Cabinet." It consists
of a finely polished cherry cabinet, containing twenty
boxes, grooved on the insides to receive twenty-five
slides each, and provided with a lock. One of these
cabinets holding 250 slides, can be gotten for only
$2,50, from Milton Bradley & Co., Springfield, Mass.
Send for their illustrated circular.

Our young ornithologists want good shot-guns.
The Parker Top-Action, breech-loader, has been
recommended to us by one who ought to know, as
one of the very best. At the International Gun
Trials, held at Bergen Point, N. J,, April 3, 1884,
" It won the admiration of all by its fine shooting
qualities. Parker Brothers, Makers, Meriden, Conn.

*Taxidermy and Entomological and Oological Sup-
plies.* After you have your birds, you may want
them mounted; and after you have your insects, you
need to pin them into cases. Ellis & Webster, Paw-
tucket, R. I.,are reliable dealers, and will either prepare your specimens for you, or put you in the way
of doing it yourself. Send for their catalogue.

Southwick & Jencks keep an excellent Natural
History store in Providence, R. I. Birdskins, eggs,
minerals, shells, supplies for Ornithologists, Taxidermists, Oologists and Botanists, including publica-
tions. Send for specimen number of their monthly,
" Random Notes on Natural History," at 50 cents
per year, and for circulars of catalogues.

Philosophical Apparatus, such as Electrical ma-
chines, Air-pumps, Magnets, Magic Lanterns, etc.,

Chemical apparatus of all sorts, and sets of Geological instruments for analysis, may be gotten of the best quality from J. & H. Berge, 191 Greenwich Street, New York City. Send for catalogue.

Frank H. Lattin, Gaines, Orleans Co., New York, is a young man who, by his unaided efforts, has built up a large and increasing trade in Birds' Eggs, Shells, Minerals, Scientific books, and Naturalists' supplies in general. His prices for eggs seem to be lower than any we have seen. Price-lists and circulars sent on application.

The Young Scientists, is the name of a firm of which Mr. C. F. Gettemy, one of our A. A. members, is an officer. They are prepared to fill orders for Taxidermists' and Naturalists' supplies. Address: Galesburg, Illinois.

For Entomological Supplies, address the Naturalists' Supply Co., Box 469, Philadelphia, Pa. They carry a large stock of Nets, Pins, Cork, Setting-blocks, Killing-jars, and everything pertaining to Entomology. Also a full line of Egg-drills, Blow-pipes, and Ornithological supplies. Price lists may be had on application.

Printing. Every Naturalist finds it convenient now and then, to have a little printing done. It may be only labels for his specimens, or exchange lists of his duplicates; or he may wish to print a monograph on some subject of investigation, or perhaps he has written a book. Chapters of A. A. often wish to see their By-laws, etc., in type. To all such we recommend as thoroughly reliable, the printers of this Hand-book, The Sun Printing Company, Pittsfield, Mass.

CHAPTER XVII.

ALPHABETICAL LIST OF CHAPTERS CLASSIFIED BY STATES.

[In the middle column, the first figures show the number of active, and the following figures, of honorary members. Under these figures, the initials show the special departments of study. The abbreviations are—

A.—Anatomy.	Ch.—Chemistry.	Mic.—Microscopy.
B.—Botany.	E.—Entomology.	Or.—Ornithology.
Bi.—Biology.	G.—Geology.	O.—Oology.
C.—Conchology.	M.—Mineralogy.	Phys.—Physiology.
	Z.—Zoology.	

The P esident's name is above the Secretary's. When only one is given it is usually that of the Secretary.]

CALIFORNIA.

No. of Chap.	Name and Address.	No. of Mem.	Pres. and Sec.
621.	Garden Grove, A.	3–1 E.	Mrs. M. E. Head. Horace C. Head.
608.	Los Gatos, A. *Santa Clara Co.*	5 E.M.Or.	Geo. Francis. E. L. Menefee.
131.	Nevada City, A.	20	Miss Maude Smith.
41.	Oakland, A. 1305 *Broadway.*	7	Henry C. Converse.
102.	Oakland, B.	5	Geo. S. Meredith.
421.	Petaluma, A.	12–1	Jonathan Green. Miss Cora Derby.
179.	Sacramento, A.	15–5 B., E.	Newton Tyburn. Chas. Mier.
166.	St. Helena, A. *Napa City.*	6 B., G.	P. S. King. Mrs. E. H. King.
49.	San Francisco, B. 1626 *Turk st.*	5	Miss M. T. Vandenburgh.
296.	San Francisco, D.	8	Sewall Dolliver. Miss Bertha L. Rowell.

6

No. of Chap.	Name and Address.	No of Mem.	Pres. and Sec.
321.	San Francisco, E. 1330 *Sutter st.*	6	Augustus B. Taylor. Wm. F. Breeze.
333.	San Francisco, F. 1416 *Sacramento st.*	12 Phys.	Miss Estelle Miller. Miss Bertha L. Rowell.
527.	San Francisco, G. 633 *Tyler st.*	6	Norman Sinclair.
335.	San Jose, A.	8	F. R. Garnier, *Box* 181.
59.	Santa Cruz, A.	2 B.	Miss C. W. Baldwin.
564.	Santa Rosa, A. *Lock box* 43.	6–1 E.Mic.M.	Louis M. King. Wilbur M. Swett.
318.	Sweetland, A.	7	Miss K. M. Fowler.

COLORADO.

584.	Col. Springs, A.	4	E. B. McMorris,—B.
122.	Denver, A. 476 *Champa st.*	6	Miss Cora Moore.
262.	Denver. B. *Box* 2272.	4	Mrs. E. M. Roberts. Ernest L. Roberts.
413.	Denver, C. *Hoyt & Delano sts.*	7–2 E.O.Or.	W. J. Denchfield. H. G. Smith, Jr.
425.	Greely, A.	7	Louis L. Haynes.
311.	San Juan, A.	5	Mrs. L. J. Brewster.

CONNECTICUT.

624.	Abington, A.	13 Z.	Miss Mary R. Allen. Miss J. E. L. Dennis.
618.	Central Village. A.	40–4	N. W. Sanborn, M. D. Miss Minnie French.
100.	Hartford, B. 55 *Prospect st.*	25–1 E., Or.	Miss Annie K. Bunce. Francis Parsons.
274.	Hartford, D. 2 *Farmington av.*	5 E.	C. H. Day. W. R. Royce.
408.	Hartford, E. 194 *Farmington av.*	12	W. H. St. John.
643.	Higganum. A.	5 E.. O., M.	Mrs. Walter N. Gay. Miss Estella E. Clark.

No. of Chap.	Name and Address.	No. of Mem.	Pres. and Sec.
354.	Litchfield, A.	4	L. B. Woodruff.
101.	Middletown, A.	10–8	John A. Dodd.
	Box 1414.		Lewis G. Westgate.
462.	New Haven, A.	13–11	H. R. Northrup.
	Skinner School.	E. M.	J. H. Haydon.
171.	New London, A.	8–7	W. D. Young.
			R. L. Crump.
616.	Norwich, A.	22–1	A. N. Burke.
	Box 1086. B. O. Or. Z.		A. L. Aiken.
237.	Plantsville, A.	7	H. C. Shepard.
257.	Plantsville, B.	9–2	G. M. Smith.
	E. B. Or.		C. H. Banning.
165.	Plymouth, A.	4–4	Joseph Langdon.
	O. Or.		W. G. Talmadge.
590.	Pomfret Centre, A.	4	Miss Emily S. Warren.
	Box 11.	B. E.	Mrs. S. O. Marsh.
637.	Putnam, A.	7	Rev. A. P. Chapman.
			H. W. Chapman.
522.	Sharon, A.	16–12	Willard Baker.
	B. E. M.		Miss C. S. Roberts.
268.	Thompsonville, A.	32	Miss Alice Briscoe.
325.	Torrington, A.	6	J. F. Alldis.
123.	Waterbury, A.	2	Edward Lampson.
	Lock box 756.		Herbert N. Johnson.
415.	Waterbury, C.	2	W. C. Carter.
	52 *Grove St.* Or. M.		

DISTRICT OF COLUMBIA.

No. of Chap.	Name and Address.	No. of Mem.	Pres. and Sec.
109.	Washington, C.	17–6	G. F. Weld.
	1600 13*th st.*, *N. W.* A.B.E.Ch.		Alonzo H. Stewart.
460.	Washington, D.	7	Vernon Dorsey.
	3038 *P st.*, *W.*	M. Z.	F. A. Reynolds.
275.	Washington, E.	4	G. Wilson Beatty.
	204 4*th st.*, *S. E.*	E.	Alonzo H. Stewart.
448.	Washington, G.	18–3	
	1727 *F st.*, *N. W.* B. E. M.		Miss Isabelle McFarland.

No. of Chap.	Name and Address.	No. of Mem.	Pres. and Sec.

DAKOTA TERRITORY.

400. Fargo, A.   14–1   Nath. Stephenson.
    E.   Frank Brown.

DELAWARE.

152. Wilmington, A.   ' 1   J. H. Rollo.
   700 *King st.*   Min.
439. Wilmington, B.   9–1   Malcolm MacLear.
   417 *Washington st.* E.M.   Percy C. Pyle.
562. Wilmington, C.   8   A. E. Keigwin.

FLORIDA.

411. Blackwater, A.   3–8   Miss Alice A. Chandler.
   B. E.   Miss Kittie C. Roberts.
567. Fort Meade, A.   5   Carl M. Keck.
   (*Formerly Sigourney, Ia.*)   Irving Keck.
22. Grahamville, A.   2   Miss Edna Pearl Lisk.

ILLINOIS.

10. Aurora, A.   3   Miss Lilian L. Trask.
108. Chicago, D.   4   D. A. French.
   Hodge's block, 22d st.   O.Or.   Ch. W. Sprague.
153. Chicago, E.   5–3   Grafton Parker.
   153 *25th st.*   E. G. Or.   E. W. Wentworth.
229. Chicago, F.   7–5   Graham Davis.
   2546 *S. Dearborn.*   All.   E. R. Larned.
313. Chicago, H.   13
   51 *S. Sheldon.*   O. J. Steiner.
342. Chicago, I.   4
   1212 *Wabash av.*   E. Shepherd.
383. Chicago, L.   6
   1236 *Wabash av.*   W. B. Jansen.
419. Chicago, M.   84–6   Geo. Lynne.
   107 *Sedgwick st.*   G.   Geo. Lynne.
523. Chicago, O.   5–6   A. W. Glover.
   334 *Monroe st.*   ,M. Z.   A. L. Baxter.

No. of Chap.	Name and Address.	No. of Mem.	Pres. and Sec.
531.	Chicago, P. 3011 *Mich. av.*	6	Harry Hirsch.
541.	Chicago, Q. 3014 *Mich. av.*	4 M.	O. E. Taft.
583.	Chicago, R. 96 *Drexel av.*	8 Mic.	W. E. Hale. G. E. Hale.
588.	Chicago. S. 41 *Aldine sq.*	7-2	W. G. Jerrems, Jr. W. A. Wilkins.
596.	Chicago, T. 50 *S. Ada st.*	6	W. L. Dawson. B. W. Peck.
603.	Chicago, U. 3120 *Calumet av.*	3 E.	C. F. McLean.
649.	Chicago, V. 242 *Bissel st.*	6-3 M. E.	Harry Crawford. Harvey Murray.
12.	Forreston, A.	5	C. M. Winston. Pare Winston.
25.	Freeport, A.	5	Miss Anne Jenkins.
388.	Galesburgh, A.	10-3 B. E. G.	E. C. Lambert. W. S. Nash.
550.	Galesburgh, B. 208 *N. Academy st.*	9-1 E. G. Or.	Ernest E. Calkins. C. F. Gettemy.
466.	Golconda, A.	13	Oscar Rauchfuss. Robert Galbraith.
365.	Hyde Park, A. *Box 292.*	24-4 Or.	Sidney H. West. E. W. Potter.
95.	Joliet, A.	16	Miss Addie W. Smith.
430.	Kinmundy, A.	5	Bertie Squire.
105.	Limerick, A.	13	John W. Jordan.
509.	Macomb, A.	10 Or.	Miss G. VanHoesen. Miss Nellie Tunnicliff.
525.	Monmouth, A.	4 B. Phys.	J. A. Dose. D. E. Waid.
641.	Normal Park, A. *Box 173.*	Or. M.	Edward Colegrove. Miss Charlotte Putnam.

No. of Chap.	Name and Address.	No. of Mem.	Pres. and Sec.
287.	Ottawa, A.	8–4	
		B. E.	Ray Hoffman.
156.	Peoria, A.	12	Edgar Eldridge.
	104 *Pa. ac.*		Tobey Van Buskirk.
184.	Peoria, B.	6	
	1142 *S. Adams st.*		Eddie Smith.
320.	Peoria, C.	6	
	211 *N. Elizabeth.*		J. A. Smith.
648.	Peoria, D.	4	Frank Cobleigh.
	302 *Moss st.*	Or.	H. J. Woodward.
346.	Princeton, A.	4	R. C. Trimble.
		M. O.	W. K. Trimble.
499.	Princeton, C.	6	Harry Bailey.
515.	Rogers Park, A.	4	Mrs. E. S. Gridley.
		E. M.	C. B. Coxe.
393.	S. Evanston. A.	17	C. B. Atwell.
		B. Bi.	Miss C. B. Adams.
65.	Wright's Grove, A.	4–2	Mrs. Brown.
	4802 *La Salle ac.*		W. B. Greenleaf.

INDIANA.

606.	Evansville, A.	5–2	Cyrus K. Drew.
	421 *Chandler ac.* E.G.Or.Z.		Clarence D. Gilchrist.
358.	Green Castle, A.	1	Joseph H. Earp.
420.	Hanover, A.	5	Box 1.
528.	Huntingsburg, A.	7	C. H. Behrens.
			Hugh C. Rothert.
145.	Indianapolis, A.	11	
	265 *E. N. Y. st.*		F. Bildenmeister.
265.	Indianapolis, B.	7	
	156 *Ash st.*		Miss Cornelia McKay.
558.	Indianapolis, C.	12	Henry Dithmer.
	303 *N. J. st.*	E.	Russell Robinson.
574.	Indianapolis, D.	8	Tom Moore.
	332 *Ala. st.*		John Schramm.

No. of Chap.	Name and Address.	No. of Mem.	Pres. and Sec.
195.	Kentland, A,	8 ·	Mrs. C. P. Boswell.
			Miss Birdie Blye.
103.	La Porte, A.	7	Frank Eliel.
426.	La Porte, B.	4	Leo B. Austin.
491.	Rochester, A.	11–1	Miss Tina Smith.
	Box S.	A.	Miss Nellie Scull.
636.	Rockville, A.	5	Edwin C. Thurston.
		M.	Miss Lilla Moore.
431.	Terre Haute, A.	17–2	Ed. Thurston.
	629 *Mulberry st.*	E.	B. M. Condit.
633.	Terre Haute, B.	7–1	Arthur McKeene.
	622 *Chestnut st.*		O. C. Mewhinney.

IOWA.

118.	Bristow, A.	1	J. B. Playter, Mic.
64.	Cedar Rapids, A.	14–21	R. C. Greene.
	3d av. & 5th st.	E. M. G.	E. P. Boynton.
330.	Cedar Rapids, B.	12–25	E. C. Clark.
		E. G.	C. R. Eastman.
551.	Clinton, A.	6	Miss Mabel E. Loveder.
	Box 486.	E.	Henry Towle.
158.	Davenport, A.	15	E. K. Putnam.
632.	Davenport, B.	6–2	
	Griswold College.		Miss Sarah G. Foote.
285.	Dubuque, A.	8	Alvin S. Wheeler.
20.	Fairfield, A.	12–23	Miss Carrie A. Lamson.
	Box 213.	E. G.	Miss Sue Blair.
514.	Iowa City, A.	5–1	H. F. Wickham.
		E. Or.	W. M. Clute.
327.	Muscatine, A.	4	Glenn A. Gordon.
578.	Osceola, A.	9	Mrs. L. E. Banta.
	Box 744.		Harlan Richards.
540.	Oskaloosa, B.	20–8	A. C. Scott.
	Box 682.		O. D. McMains.
15.	Ottumwa, A.	21–35	Miss Belle Foster.
			W. R. Lighton.

No. of Chap.	Name and Address.	No. of Mem.	Pres. and Sec.
546.	Palo, A.	10	Miller Barnhill.
56.	Pine Croft.	6	Miss Lida Price.
	Greene.		Miss Lavenia Price.
233.	Sydney, A.	4	Mrs. W. H. Trites.
		B. M. Z.	Mr. Geo. Trites.
547.	Shellsburg, A.	25	O. H. Thompson.
238.	Winterset, A.	3	Mott Wheelock.
		M.	Harry Wallace.

KANSAS.

No. of Chap.	Name and Address.	No. of Mem.	Pres. and Sec.
225.	Burlington, A.	4	A. M. Hendee.
		O. Or. E.	P. M. Floyd.
304.	Emporia, A.	10	
	Box 1186.		L. O. Perley.
292.	Independence. A.	18	W. H. Plank.
519.	Lawrence, A.	5	F. H. Bowersock.
597.	Lawrence, B.	10–4	Pliny Allen.
	Box 89.	E. O. M.	Albert Garret.
142.	Leavenworth, A.	14	W. L. Burrell.
	327 *Delaware st.*		
526.	Leavenworth, B.	9–1	W. P. Brown.
	616 *Walnut st.*	B. O. G.	H. P. Johnson.
270.	Severance. A.	9	W. S. Franklin.
301.	Topeka, A.	5	
	218 *Polk st.*		C. A. Dailey.
308.	Wellington. A.	5	
	Box 504.		J. T. Nixon.

KENTUCKY.

No. of Chap.	Name and Address.	No. of Mem.	Pres. and Sec.
207.	Bowling Green, A.	3–1	J. W. Durkee.
		G.	Miss Jessie Glenn.
133.	Erlanger, A.	5	Alex. Bedinger.
			L. M. Bedinger.

MAINE.

No. of Chap.	Name and Address.	No. of Mem.	Pres. and Sec.
332.	Augusta, A.	10–2	Mrs. H. A. Hall.
	Box 231.		G. C. Libby.

No. of Mem.	Name and Address.	No. of Mem.	Pres. and Sec.
443.	Brunswick, A.	6	E. B. Young.
263.	Gardner, A.	14	A. C. Brown.
484.	Oldtown. A.	6	Miss Mabel Waldron.
651.	Portland, A.	4	P. E. Perry.
	717 *Congress st.* E. M. Or.		W. H. Dow.
444.	Rockland, A.	11	J. P. Cilley, Jr.
		B. N. H.	Miss Grace T. Cilley.
468.	Saco, C.	18	Edward Goshen.
	Care L. F. Bradbury.		Miss Genie Preble.
442.	Waldoboro, A.	5	Allen R. Benner—E. & G.
138.	Warren, A.		L. J. Hills.
		B. G.	A. M. Hilt.
465.	Waterville, A.	8-3	C. B. Wilson.
		E. O. Or.	C. W. Spencer.

MARYLAND.

635.	Annapolis, A.	6-1	Harry C. Hopkins.
	St. John's College. E. O. M.		A. H. Hopkins.
7.	Baltimore, A.	1	J. H. Hughes,238 Mad.av.
73.	Baltimore, B.	6-12	Miss H. C. Allnutt.
	76 *Md. ar.*		Miss Susie H. Keith.
368.	Baltimore, D.	6	
	223 *Md. ar.*		Miss Fannie Wyatt.
387.	Baltimore, E.	15-2	Miss Rebecca F. Clark.
	2 *Denmead st.* Or. B. Phys.		Helen C. Coale.
480.	Baltimore, F.	12-1	Miss M. Reinhardt.
	222 *McCulloh st.* E.		Miss R. Jones.
614.	Baltimore, II.	8-2	J. B. Rollins.
	211 *Presstman st.* B. M.		R. S. Hart.
598.	St. George's, A.	17-2	C. H. T. Lowndes.
	Reistertown P. O. B.		Mrs. Mary B. Kinear.

MASSACHUSETTS.

149.	Abington, A.	12-1	E. W. Blake.
			C. A. Cushman.

No. of Chap.	Name and Address.	No. of Mem.	Pres. and Sec.
352.	Amherst, A.	18–2 E. B. Or.	W. B. Greenough. Miss E. S. Field.
379.	Andover, B. Box 341.	5	
348.	Ashland, A. Box 174.	20–7	W. G. Whittemore.
24.	Boston, A. 52 Woodbine st.	6–1 B. M.	A. P. Stone. F. A. North.
162.	Boston, B. 99 Revere st.	2 Z.	A. C. Chamberlain.
367.	Boston, C. 47 Concord sq.	4	Miss Alice M. Gay. Miss Annie Darling.
496.	Boston, E. Olney st., Ward 24.	6	G. A. Orrok.
593.	Brookline, A.	6 E. B. Or. M.	Geo. L. Briggs.
224.	Cambridgeport, B.	5	F. L. Hammond.
390.	Chester, A.	20	Rev. A. E. Todd. Wm. Stanton.
629.	Chicopee, A. Box 200.	24 B. M. Z.	R. E. Bemis. Miss E. L. Mitchell.
658.	Chicopee, B.	10	A. C. Towne. Miss E. B. Bullens.
218.	Clinton, A.	10	Gerald Alley.
516.	Dighton, A.	16	W. A. Reade.
429.	Dorchester, A. 15 Columbia st.	10–2	W. H. Tenney, Jr. Miss Miriam Badlam.
261.	E. Boston, A. 118 Lexington st.	10 Z.	Miss Emma Bates. Miss Ruth A. Odiorne.
351.	E. Boston, B. 203 Saratoga st.	25	W. D. Clark.
143.	E. Bridgewater, A.	5	G. S. Young.
545.	Fall River, A. Box 275.	8	F. H. Young. O. K. Hawes.
48.	Fitchburgh, A.	4 B. E.	J. W. Richmond. A. B. Simonds.

No. of Chap.	Name and Address.	No. of Mem.	Pres. and Sec.
173.	Fitchburg, B.	13–3	F. J. Perkins. Miss Mary Garfield.
201.	Fitchburg, C.	12–2	Thornton M. Ware. Miss Ellen A. Snow.
450.	Fitchburg, D. Box 1335.	13 Z.	G. V. Upton. G. F. Whittemore.
642.	Florence, A. Box 22.	23 Or. M.	Prof. G. A. Hoadly. A. T. Bliss.
282.	Greenfield, A.	6	Prof. C. H. K. Sanderson.
579.	Hadley, A. Box 229.	6 G. Or.	Miss Julia Dwight. Miss Mary A. Cook.
458.	Haverhill, A. 2 Arch st.	2	F. H. Chase.
217.	Hyde Park, A. Box 405.	14	
124.	Jamaica Plain, A. Glen Road.	4 G. Or. M.	R. W. Wood, Jr. G. W. Wheelwright, Jr.
1.	Lenox, A. Box 178.	10–6 220*	Oakleigh Thorne. H. H. Ballard.
210.	Lowell, B. Box 155.	7	G. A. Whitmore.
586.	Lowell, C. 127 Nesmith st.	5 M. Z.	C. S. Hutchinson. H. C. Rogers.
297.	Malden, A. Box 131 Faulkner.	6	C. C. Beale.
111.	Milford, A. Box 643.	5	C. F. Hicks.
72.	Needham, A.	7	Gilbert Mann.
281.	Newburyport, B.	6	R. E. Curtis.
411.	New Salem, A.	' 1	D. F. Carpenter.
481.	Newton, A.	12–10 Z.	E. L. Douglass. F. M. Elms.
47.	Newton Centre, A.	4	John Bond. Philip Britchett.

*Corresponding members.

No. of Chap.	Name and Address.	No. of Mem.	Pres. and Sec.
256.	Newton Up. Falls, A.	7–3	J. F. Hopkins.
	B. M. Or.		Miss Josie M. Hopkins.
355.	N. Adams, A.	13–3	Miss E. H. Brewer.
	B. G. Z.		Miss Louise Radlo.
17.	Northampton, A.	3–4	M. Allie Maynard.
			Miss Florence Maynard
435.	Northampton, B.	4	
	Box 756.		H. L. Hilliard.
170.	N. Brookfield, A.	13	E. P. Jenks.
	Box 310.		H. A. Cooke.
92.	N. Cambridge, A.	4	H. A. Seagrave.
		E.	F. E. Keay.
492.	Peru, A.	6	C. B. Cone.
		B. E.	Miss Hyla A. Stowell.
60.	Pigeon Cove, A.	11–4	C. C. Fears.
		M.	C. H. Andrews.
183.	Salem, A.	5	M. E. Burrill.
	4 Cherry st.		
438.	Somerville, A.	6	Harry G. Sears.
112.	S. Boston, A.	11	W. O. Hersey.
	37 Gates st.	N. H.	H. E. Sawyer.
212.	S. Boston, B.	4–4	G. H. Chittenden.
	729 E. 4th st.	M. O. Or.	H. C. Clapp.
580.	S. Boston, C.	5–3	P. C. Sheldon.
	777 B'y.	E. M.	F. M. Spaulding.
617.	S. Williamstown, A.	27	N. P. Goodell.
	Greylock Inst.	B. M. Or.	R. C. Campbell.
575.	Spencer, A.	14–5	G. A. Drury.
			Miss May B. Ladd.
500.	Stockbridge, A.		Miss Bessie Chaffee.
219.	Taunton, B.	18–5	Miss Edith Lovering.
		E. Or. M.	A. C. Bent.
66.	Waltham, A.	7	
	Box 1339.		H. Hancock.
269.	Wareham, A.	11–1	Miss Alice M. Guernsey.
	High School.	M.	G. W. Dempsey.

No. of Mem.	Name and Address.	No. of Mem.	Pres. and Sec.
338.	Wareham, B.	6–3	Arthur Hammond.
281.	Webster, A.	4	R. G. Leavitt.
464.	Westboro, A.	30	Miss Kitty A. Gage.
189.	W. Medford, A.	2	Miss Isabel G. Dame.
	Box 197.	B. E.	Miss Gertrude Dame.

MICHIGAN.

No.	Name and Address	No. of Mem.	Pres. and Sec.
384.	Ann Arbor, A.	6	D. H. Browne.
328.	Buchanan, A.	4	Willie Talbot.
14.	Detroit, A.	16	A. S. Wiley.
		E.	Miss Bertha Wiley.
120.	Detroit, B.	8	
	62 *Miami av.*		Miss Ella M. Leggett.
157.	Detroit, C.	8–7	George W. Kelley.
	26 *Henry st.*		E. M. Raynale.
652.	Dowagiac, A.	11–4	V. M. Tuthill.
		E.	E. F. Perry.
50.	Flint, A.	1	
	Box 1425.		Miss H. A. Lovell.
71.	Grand Rapids, A.	4	Willie G. Allyn.
571.	Grand Rapids, B.	15	Geo. C. Hollister.
	Old Nat. Bank.	Or. M. E.	Louis Carpenter.
135.	Jackson, A.	17–4	E. D. Warner.
	228 *Main st.*		J. O. D. Bennett.
164.	Jackson, B.	17	
	Cor. Main & 4th sts.		Mrs. Norah Gridley.
96.	Lansing, A.	6	Rodman H. Cary.
		M.	James P. Edmonds.
569.	Ludington, A.	15	Ch. T. Sawyer.
626.	Petoskey, A.	10–2	Mrs. Watson Snyder.
		O. Or.	W. B. Lawton.
607.	Union City, A.	9	Miss Minnie Drum.
			Carl Spencer.
237.	Ypsilanti, B.	2–1	Louis B. Hardy, E. G.

No. of Chap.	Name and Address.	No. of Mem.	Pres. and Sec.
		MINNESOTA.	
26.	Detroit City, A.	5	C. C. Dix.
542.	Faribault, A.	10	Miss Eva Whipple.
	St. Mary's Hall.		Miss E. M. Blythe.
178.	Farmington, A.	8	H. N. Wing.
117.	Minneapolis, A.	20	
	1816 *Fourth av.*	N.	Miss Jennie Hughes.
194.	Minneapolis, B.	7	
	1016 *Western av.*		Burtie W. McCracken.
386.	Pine City, A.	4	E. L. Stephan.
		B. E.	Miss L. M. Stephan.
121.	St. Paul, A.	14–1	Mrs. J. DeGraw.
			Frank Ramaley.
139.	St. Paul, B	6	
	54 *Davidson block.*		Sidney E. Farwell.
428.	St. Paul, C.	6	
	5 *Laurel av.*		P. C. Allen.
369.	St. Paul, D.	6	
	Box 5.		Fred Spaulding.
565.	Waseca, A.	6	E. A. Everett.
	Box 128.		J. F. Murphy.
		MISSISSIPPI.	
573.	Moss Point, A.	12	Miss Bessie Borden.
544.	Oxford, A.	6–2	Mrs. M. L. Hutson.
			C. Woodward Hutson.
601.	West Point, A.	16–5	Judge B. F. Owen.
		E. Z.	R. S. Cross.
		MISSOURI.	
276.	Kansas City, A.	6	
	114 *W. 6th st.*		F. M. Pease.
634.	Macon, A.	5	Maj. A. C. Longden.
	Box 876.	G. Z.	Lieut. C. W. Kimball.
33.	St. Louis, A.	4	Wm. S. Love.
	1818 *Wash. st.*	M.	Miss Maud M. Love.

No. of Chap.	Name and Address.	No. of Mem.	Pres. and Sec.
46.	St. Louis, B. 1233 *N. 20th st.*	2	H. B. Crucknell. C. F. Haanel.
202.	St. Louis, C. 1014 *Cass av.*	12	Miss L. M. Follet.
638.	St. Louis, D. 3857 *Wash. av.* M. G. E.	7	W. C. Watts. Frank M. Davis.
366.	Webster Groves, A. *Box* 113.	39	Edwin R. Allen.

NEW HAMPSHIRE.

No.	Name and Address	Mem.	Pres. and Sec.
587.	Concord, A. *Box* 421.	4–2 G. B.	Rev. H. P. Lamprey. Miss Lunette E. Lamprey.
440.	Keene, A. *Box* 307.	6–1 E.	H. S. Foster. F. H. Foster.
391.	Meredith, A. *N. Sanbornton.*	10–1 B.	H. M. Robinson. Ch. F. Robinson.
21.	Nashua, A. *Box* 757. E. Bi. Or. M.	13–27	J. W. Thurber. F. W. Greeley.
125.	Nashua, C.	4	Charles Howard.
181.	Nashua, E.	1 M.	Geo. M. Tinkei.
294.	Swanzey, A. *Marlboro Depot.*	4	Miss L. A. Whitcomb.

NEW JERSEY.

No.	Name and Address	Mem.	Pres. and Sec.
518.	Bergen Point, A. *Box* 69.	5	Miss Alida Conover.
372.	Beverley, A. *Box* 88.	7–4 E.	H. B. Carpenter. Miss Alice T. Carpenter.
373.	Beverley, B. *Box* 14.	6–4	J. P. Street. P. S. Clarkson.
437.	Burlington, A.	4	Natalie McNeal.
560.	Cambridge, A. *Riverside, box* 19. E. C. M.	10	Miss M. M. McGonigal. G. Morrison Taylor.
113.	Camden, A. 307 *N. 3d st.*	6	Miss Mabel Adams.

No. of Mem.	Name and Address.	No. of Mem.	Pres. and Sec.
548.	Crawford, A. *Box* 106.	6–1	Miss Katie Ells. Miss Maud A. Cox.
461.	East Orange, A. *Brick Church P. O.*	12–4	Miss Sarah R. Adams. Miss Stella L. Hook.
605.	East Orange, B. *Grovestend.*	5–2 E. M.	F. H Chandler. Alfred E. Horan.
570.	Hackensack, A. O. B. M. Z. Or.	4	A. J. Voorhis. Philander Betts.
417	Keyport, A. B. Z.	7	Wm. Van Geison. Phelps Cherry.
349.	Linden, A.	6	E. H. Schram.
640.	Milville, A. Or.	9	Herbert Westwood. Carder Hazard.
639.	Montclair, A. *Box* 147. B. Z.	6–6	Marion Bedell. Miss Lucy B. Parsons.
74.	Moorestown, A. *Box* 115.	7	Miss Anna F. Thomas.
337.	Newark, A. 164 *Mulberry st.* Or. O. E.	9–5	Fred. W. Neiman. Chas, Wegle.
403.	Newark, B. 687 *Broad st.* Or.	2–3	Frank Lynch. Chas. Barrows.
572.	Newark, C. 611 *High st.* E. M. O. B.	10	Max Farrand. L. M. Passmore.
249.	Orange, A.		Geo. M. Smith.
423.	Perth Amboy, A. Z. B.	30–5	Miss Bessie Yocom. Miss Bertha Mitchell.
398.	Roseville, A.	20	Sara Darrach.
13.	Trenton. A. 154 *W. State st.* B.	8–1	Miss Anna B. Newbold. Miss M. S. McIlvaine.
497.	Trenton. B. *Box* 424. A. O. E. M.	4–3	Harry Archer. Joseph Archer.
543	Washington, A. *Lock box* 6.	5	Mrs. Wm. M. Baird. Dr. Wm. M. Baird.

No. of Chap.	Name and Address.	No. of Mem.	Pres. and Sec.

NEW YORK.

187.	Albany, A.	6–2	F. P. Huested.
	3 *LaFayette st.*	E.	John P. Gavit.
288.	Albany, B.	7	
	10 *Hawk st.*		Wm. R. Nichols.
457.	Albany, C.	7–8	J. P. Ryan.
	240 *Clinton av.*		W. L. Martin.
226.	Alfred Centre, A.	16	C. A. Davis.
114.	Auburn, A.	8	
	7 *Franklin st.*		Miss Mamie L. Kimberly.
336.	Auburn, B.	12	J. L. Hickok.
	13 *Aurelius av.*		E. L. Hickok.
476.	Aurora, A.	27	E. L. French.
559.	Bath, A.	4–2	Friend Miller.
	Steuben Co.	Z. E.	Percy C. Meserve.
645.	Bath, B.	6–3	W. H. Chamberlain.
	M. E. Or. B.		Chas. L. Kingsley.
295.	Boonville, A.	3	S. W. Nelson.
		G.	F. C. Johnson.
19.	Brooklyn, A.	7	
	171 *Clinton st.*		Miss Lucy Tupper.
82.	Brooklyn, B.	6–2	James M. Patten.
	11 *Garden pl.*	Z. M.	Chas. B. Davenport.
364.	Brooklyn, D.	3–1	Harry Ager.
	6 *St. James place.*	M. B.	J. N. Drake.
374.	Brooklyn, E.	11	F. N. Cheshire.
	136 *7th st.* Z. B. G. C.		Frank E. Cocks.
382.	Brooklyn, F.	8–9	Miss Alice Van Ingen.
	135 *Henry st.*	G. E.	Dudley A. Van Ingen.
422.	Brooklyn, G.	9	John Walsh.
	98 *2d place.*	B. Z.	R. C. Avery, Jr.
609.	Brooklyn, H.	10	Miss Alice Van Ingen.
	122 *Remsen st.*		Philip Van Ingen.
91.	Buffalo, A.	22–8	H. A. Stahl.
	960 *Wash st.* B. E. Or.		Miss C. Freeman.

7

No. of Chap.	Name and Address.	No of Mem.	Pres. and Sec.
132.	Buffalo, B. 117 14*th st.*	14-2 Arch. G. E.	A. W. Thayer. Chas. W. Dobbins.
168.	Buffalo, C. 3 *Cottage st.*	5 B. Phys.	Miss Eva Smith. Miss Jennie K. Doyle.
228.	Buffalo, D. 103 *Tremont pl.*	9	Percy Scharff.
317.	Buffalo, E. 523 *Main st.*	10	W. L. Koester.
493.	Buffalo, F. 105 14*th st.*	18-1 B. M. E.	A. C. Brown. Miss Clara A. Manser.
529.	Buffalo, H. 44 *No. Pearl st.*	7	Miss Margaret Evans.
585.	Buffalo, I. *Box* 185.	11-1	Jos. C. Pfeiffer. F. M. Moody.
334.	Chappaqua, A.	4	M. Wright Barnum.
447.	Chittenango, A.	8-4	John Flaherty. Chas. A. Jenkins.
137.	Clyde, A.	6	Geo. S. Morley, O.
478.	Comstocks, A.	4	Miss L. B. Culver. Geo. C. Baker.
479.	Durhamville, A.	5	Arthur Fox.
146.	Ellington, A.	20	W. H. Van Allen.
513.	Far Rockaway, A. *Long Island.*	8	L. I. Carleton.
150.	Flushing, A. *Long Island.*	2-1	Mrs. F. R. L. Heaton. Miss F. M. L. Heaton.
604.	Fredonia, A.	6 B. E.	Miss Mary E. Bemis. Mrs. Jennie N. Curtis.
254.	Fulton, A.	3-1 C.	C. Bennett. H. C. Howe.
294.	Garden City, A. *Long Island.*	4	Dr. J. S. Hawley. Wm. R. Kitchen.
186.	Geneva, A.	39	Lansing Stebbins. Miss Nellie A. Wilson.

No. of Chap.	Name and Address.	No. of Mem.	Pres. and Sec.
594.	Granville, A.	7-2	E. L. Smith.
	Box 72 N. Granville. G.O.B.Z.E.		James E. Rice.
502.	Herkimer, A.	8-1	Peter F. Piper.
		Or.	Geo. W. Nellis, Jr.
172.	Hoosac, A.	12	
	Box 53.		Miss F. G. Langdon.
625.	Hudson, A.	4-1	H. W. George.
		M. G. Or.	Robt. E. Terry.
89.	Hull's Mills, A.	7	
	Dutchess Co.		Miss Alice Brower.
37.	Kingsboro, A.	12	
	Fulton Co.		M. W. Thomas.
106.	Lebanon Springs, A.	7	Mrs. M. K. Harrison.
			W. H. Harrison.
85.	Leroy, A.	13	
		M.	Miss C. A. Talmage.
79.	Lockport, A.	140	Geo. W. Pound.
563.	Lyons, A.	6-2	Charlie Ennis.
	Box 428.	G. O.W.	Leroy Ostrander.
620.	Manlius, A.	10-4	Robt. W. Bowman.
	St. John's.		Geo. C. Beebe.
623.	Manlius, B.	9	
	St. John's.		C. H. Cuyler.
556.	Moravia, A.	6	Chas. L. Atwood.
			F. S. Curtis.
144.	Mt. Vernon, A.	12	Aubrey Tyson.
503.	Nassau, A.	6	Miss Emily P. Sherman.
252.	Nanuet, A.	3-2	C. Hasbrouck Wells.
	Box 19.	Or. M. G.	Oscar D. Dike.
67.	New York, A.	4	
	12 Lexington av.		James Robb.
87.	New York, B.	18-2	A. C. Rudischhauser.
	244 Madison st.		Edward B. Miller.
116.	New York, D.	5-2	Albert Tuska.
	223 E. 18th st.	Mic. B.	Gustav R. Tuska.

No. of Chap.	Name and Address.	No. of Mem.	Pres. and Sec.
161.	New York, E. 224 W. 34th st.	4	C. R. Burke.
191.	New York, F. 51 E. 44th st.	2	H. L. Mitchell. Bucknor Van Amringe.
234.	New York, G. 335 W. 27th st.	3 G. E.	R. Moeller. F. W. Roos.
312.	New York, H. 249 W. 26th st.	2	Edward Hesse. Geo. Wildey.
407.	New York, J. 120 Broadway.		A. C. Weeks.
414.	New York, K. 139 W. 49th st.	6	Heinrich Ries.
477.	New York, M. 200 W 57th st.	5	A. C. P. Opdyke.
490.	New York, N. 670 E. 142d st.	10 E. Phys.	Stephen D. Sammis. Stephen D. Sammis.
592.	New York, P. 1101 Lexington av.	4 E.	H. A. Elsberg. C. Elsberg.
630.	New York, Q. 106 Varick st.	4	J. C. Rowe. W. T. Demarest.
595.	Oneonta, A.	4 B. As.	Miss N. S. Van Woret. Miss Jessie E. Jenks.
453.	Oswego, A.	7	W. A. Burr.
504.	Oswego. B. 108 W. 7th st.	28	Miss Alice T. Weed.
316.	Palmyra, A.	8	Jarvis Merick.
243.	Peekskill, B.	7	Austin D. Mabie.
308.	Peekskill, C. Box 465.	7-8 M. E.	Gilbert H. Anderson. Geo. E. Briggs.
506.	Port Henry, A.	5 M. Or.	John Witherbee. John Thomas.
2.	Potsdam, A.	6	Miss Annie Usher.
491.	Rochester. A. Box 8.	11-1 A.	Miss Tina Smith. Miss Nellie Scull.

No. of Chap.	Name and Address.	No. of Mem.	Pres. and Sec.
454.	Rochester, B. 263 *N. St. Paul st.*	10 E. Or.	Miss Cornelia M. Ely.
577.	Rochester, C. *Box 604.*	12-1 Or.	Miss Bessie Kingman. Charley Boswell.
579.	Roxbury, A. *Box 85.*	10 E.	Arthur Bonton. Henry G. Cartwright.
409.	Sag Harbor, A. *Lock box 44.*	12-5. B.	Ivon C. Byram. Cornelius R. Sleight.
530.	St. Johnland, A. *Suffolk Co.*	· 4-1 E.	John H. Hennessey. Wm. H. White.
396.	Springville, A.	8	E. Everett Stanbro.
286.	Stockport, A.	13-5	Albert E. Heard. Willard J. Fisher.
412.	Syracuse, C.	8	B. Burrett Nash.
215.	Tioga Centre, A. " *The Oaks.*"	4 B. E.	A. R. Latimer. Miss Angie Latimer.
507.	Tonawanda, A.	5	Miss Maud Hittel. Miss Jennie Faulkner.
533.	Troy, A. *52 4th st.*	7	Eugene A. Darling. Robert Cluett, Jr.
232.	Utica, A. 11 *Court st.*	45-1 E. B. M. C.	C. Baker. Miss Frances E. Newland.
622.	Utica, B. *52 Spring st.*	5 G. Z.	Wm. C. White. Benj. C. George.
51.	Utopia, A.	9-2 B.	Robt. E. Kenyon. S. Oila Willard.
299.	Watertown, A. *Care Hon. A. W. Clark.*	5	Nicoll Ludlow.
272.	Westtown, A.	7	Lloyd Fisher. W. Evans.
659.	Williamsville, A. *Erie Co.*	6	N. S. Hopkins. H. E. Herr.

NEW MEXICO.

No. of Chap.	Name and Address.	No. of Mem.	Pres. and Sec.
483.	Albuquerque, A. *Box 91.*	12-5 G. C. Z. B. M.	E. C. Hall. Miss M. E. Whitcomb.

No. of Chap.	Name and Address.	No. of Mem.	Pres. and Sec.

NEVADA.

306. Belmont, A.   30   C. L. Deady.

NORTH CAROLINA.

30. Newberne. A. ·   16
    Care Geo. Allen & Co.   Mrs. E. C. Gaskins.
535. Chapel Hill, A.   6–4   Wm. J. Battle.
                                     B. E.   Miss Clara J. Martin.

OHIO,

185. Ashtabula. A.   14   Miss Nellie A. Prentice.
                                           Miss May H. Prentice.
310. Belpre, A.   5   Miss Fannie Rathbone.
· 485. Brooklyn Village, A.   32–2   W. P. Cope.
                                     B. E.   Miss Helen E. Barnard.
323. Bryan. ·A.   6   R. Kophendorfer.
                                           Miss Ethel Gillis.
302. Cincinnati, A.   3   Wm. H. Crane
    35½ Sherman ar.   E.   Gaylord Miles.
561. Cincinnati, B.   8   Alphonse Heuck.
    21 Ohio ar.   J. A. Giebel.
147. Cleveland. A.   6
    768 Harkness ar.   F. Kendall.
589. Cleveland, B.   90   A. J. Marvin.
    501 Franklin ar.   E.   Miss Josie Grannis.
307. Columbus, A.   5
    135 Park st.   E. G. Rice.
361. Columbus, B.   8   Chas. G. Smith.
196. Dayton, A.   24   Miss Abbie L. Dyer.
463. Dayton, B.   6   E. H. Faurer.
    233 Commercial st.   Jas. H. Jones.
553. Defiance, A. .   9–2   Emmet Slough.
    Lock box 234.   Emmett B. Fisher.
128. Eaton, A.   4–1   G. E. Rensman.
                                         E   W. E. Loy.
566. Elmore, A.   11   Fred. W. Jaeger.
    Box 100.   G. H. Rymers.

No. of Chap.	Name and Address.	No. of Mem.	Pres. and Sec.
631.	Fremont, A.	10–3	D. S. Gessner.
	Box 327.	Or. M.	V. D. Butman.
371.	Granville, A.	6	Miss Ida M. Saunders.
445.	Hamilton, A.	10	Rev. E. W. Abbey.
	Box 198.		E. M. Traber.
154.	Jefferson, A.		
	Ashtabula Co.		Miss Clara L. Northway.
537.	Mansfield, A.	11	D. J. W. Craig.
	78 *W. Bloom st.*	E.	E. Wilkinson, Jr.
655.	New Lynne, A.	7	G. O. Beede.
			W. H. Cook.
650.	Sandusky, A.	7–3	Fred Marshall.
	418 *Franklin st.*		John Youngs.
160.	Toledo, A.	12	Clarence C. McKecknie.
	409 *Ontario st.* G. Z. B.		Miss Katherine Scott.
360.	Urbana, A.	9–2	Jno. C. Moses.
	Lock box 857.		Wm. V. Moses.
581.	Urbana, B.	7–2	Murray Allison.
	Drawer 3.		Samuel Stone.
612,	Urbana, C.	13	E. M. S. Houston.
129.	Zanesville, A.	6	Miss Lulu Lillibridge.

OREGON.

340.	Portland, B.	15–3	Miss Lizzie Ley.
	395 4*th st.*	B.	H. W. Cardwell.

PENNSYLVANIA.

277.	Altoona, A.	10–5	Geo. Piper.
	(*Prst.*) *Box* 384.		W. C. Boult.
378.	Ambler, A.	48–2	W. Warren Funk.
		M.	Miss Jessie P. Smith.
455.	Bedford, A.	1	W. C. Langdon, Jr.
11.	Berwyn, A.	7–1	J. F. Glosser.
	Chester Co.		Miss Carrie H. Glosser.
246.	Bethlehem, A.	14–2	Harry L. Walters.
	Box 706. Or. E. B. M.		Harry Wilbur.

No. of Chap.	Name and Address.	No. of Mem.	Pres. and Sec.
599.	Bethlehem, B.	4–1	Herman S. Borhck.
	Box 401. Or. M. B. C.		Eric Doolittle.
300.	Bryn Mawr, A.	12	
	Rosemont. Or. B.		Miss Mary R. Garrett.
289.	Cambria Station, A.	6–4	Mrs. S. L. Oberholtzer.
	Or. C.		Ellis P. Oberholtzer.
255.	Chester, A.	5	Frank R. Gilbert.
136.	Columbia, A.	23	Ewing Mifflin.
			Alex. R. Craig.
190.	Duncannon, A.	12	Miss Annie J. Jackson.
279.	Easton, A.	4–1	W. Fred Keller.
	131ö *Ferry st.* G. B.		Augustus A. Tyler.
3.	Frankford, A.	76	John Shallcross.
	4701 *Leiper st. (Phila.)* E. M.		Robert T. Taylor.
326.	Freeland, A.	11	Saml. Caskey.
200.	Germantown, B.	23–19	Joseph Head.
	123 *Price st.* G. Z.		Franklin Bache.
582.	Germantown, C.	3–1	Miss Zuell Preston.
	127 *W. Penn. st.* A. Phys.		Miss Ada M. Wheeler.
489.	Gettysburg, A.	2–1	H. A. Stewart, M. Z. E.
482.	Buckingham, A.	18	J. Willis Atkinson.
	Holicong.		Miss Elizabeth Lloyd.
472.	Hazleton, A.	4–2	J. Edward Waaser.
	Luzerne Co. G. E.		Thos. F. McNair.
314.	Lancaster, A.	5–2	Theo. B. Appel.
	322 *W. James st.* E.Ch.		Edw. R. Heitshu.
397.	Mansfield Valley, A.	3–1	J. L. Prestley, G.
434.	Meadville, A.	9–3	Miss Harriet Reitze.
	Box 39. B. E.		Miss Laurena Streit.
568.	Meadville, B.	8	C. F. Weber.
	Box 29. Or. M. E.		Frank L. Armstrong.
260.	Mercer, A.	4	Mrs. H. M. Magoffin.
240.	New Milford, A.	1	W. D. Ainey.
169.	Norristown, A.	40–3	A. D. Eisenhower.
	E. B. M.		Wm. White.

No. of Mem.	Name and Address.	No. of Mem.	Pres. and Sec.
36.	Philadelphia, B. 1015 *Vine st.*	8–1	Ed. R. Graham. H. Taylor Rogers.
36.	Philadelphia, C. 1926 *N. 11th st.*	7	Miss Eleanor J. Crew.
58.	Philadelphia, D. 1314 *Franklin st.*	6–1 E.	Milton J. Rosenau. Joseph McFarland.
140.	Philadelphia, E. 5103 *Germantown av.*		Elliston J. Perot.
126.	Philadelphia, F. 2014 *Ridge av.*	1 M.	Raymond P. Kaign.
197.	Philadelphia, G. *Flourtown.*	5	B. Sliser.
198.	Philadelphia, H 2016 *Arch st.*	6	W. R. Nichols.
242.	Philadelphia, I. 1127 *Mt. Vernon st.*	4 M.B.	Albert Hill. J. Frank Stevens.
353.	Philadelphia, K. 1728 *Park av.*	8–3	Henry Kiersted. Wm. Yerker.
385.	Philadelphia, L. 1723 *N. 22d st.*	8	C. R. Woodruff.
394.	Philadelphia, M. 1823 *Vine st.*	4	Isaac Ford.
459.	Philadelphia, N. 1520 *Wilmington st.*	4	Harry Colby.
501.	Philadelphia, O. 625 *N. 15th st.*		Mrs. E. P. McCormick.
539.	Philadelphia, West, P. 3406 *Hamilton st.*	23	Robt. R. Truitt. Chas. M. List.
554.	Philadelphia, Q. 2229 *Mt. Vernon st.*	9	C. D. Harris. J. Edgar McKee.
556.	Philadelphia, R. 2206 *Green st.*	6–2	Edw. J. Wheelock. Paul T. Brown.
557.	Philadelphia, S. 1704 *Pine st.*	7 E. Z.	Wm. Walter. Miss Bessie P. Pearsall.
619.	Philadelphia, T. 520 *N. 21st st.*	5–1 B.	Jas. A. Brown. Jas. McMichael.

No. of Chap.	Name and Address.	No. of Mem.	Pres. and Sec.
644.	Philadelphia, U. 470 *N. 7th st.*	4	Mrs. E. M. Ickes. Martin Knabe, Jr.
27.	Pittsburgh, A. 5*th ar., East End.*	2 E. Phys.	Mrs. Rachel H. Mellon. Miss Mary McM. Jones.
273.	Pittsburgh, B. 20*th and Sidney sts.*	30	F. K. Gearing.
278.	Pittsburgh, East, C.	4	J. F. McCune.
298.	Pittsburgh, D. 23*d and Liberty sts.*	10	E. H. Henderson.
498.	Pittsburgh, E. 23*d & Liberty.*	3–1 M. G.	Chas. A. Creegan. Wm. H. Searight.
258.	Reading, A. *Hawthorne.*	25–17	W. E. Howe. Miss Helen B. Baer.
266.	St. Clair, A.	30–54	James Carter. Miss Mary Burwell.
532.	Sewickley, A. *Box 41.*	14–2	Miss Eva T. Miller. Marshall A. Christy.
206.	State College, A.	5–1 E. B. O.	J. Price Jackson. Geo. C. McKee.
591.	Tioga, A. *Box 255.*	17 B. M.	Miss Winnie Smith. Herbert Requa.
141.	Titusville, A.	5 B. O.	F. S. Bates. Chas. G. Carter.
199.	Wellsboro, A.	11	Miss Mary Rockwell. Miss Margaret S. Potter.
231.	Wiconisco, A.	6	J. R. Englebert.

RHODE ISLAND.

No. of Chap.	Name and Address.	No. of Mem.	Pres. and Sec.
188.	Newport, A. 15 *Park st.*	4	Fred. J. Cotton. Clark Burdick.
362.	Newport, B. 15 *Ayrault st.*	4 Or.	Frank Holt. Thos. Crosby, Jr.
615.	Newport, C. 15 *Park st.*	6 E.	Jos. R. P. Weaver. Jos. P. Cotton.
653.	Providence, C. 65 *John st.*	4–4 E. O. M. G.	W. A. Dyer. F. S. Phillips.
182.	Warren, A.	5–2 G. M.	N. R. Hall. Miss Mary Merchant.

No. of Chap.	Name and Address.	No. of Mem.	Pres. and Sec.

TENNESSEE.

No. of Chap.	Name and Address.	No. of Mem.	Pres. and Sec.
55.	Nashville, A.	20	
	117 *Monroe st.*	.	R. I. Tucker.

TEXAS.

No. of Chap.	Name and Address.	No. of Mem.	Pres. and Sec.
433.	Dallas, A.	6	D. G. Hinckley.
406.	Fort Elliot, A.	5	
	Care Capt. Hood.		Thos. S. Hood.
600.	Galveston, A.	5–3	Miss Anna L. Tucker. ·
	Ar. P and 36th st. C. B. E.		Philip C. Tucker, Jr.
32.	San Antonio, A.	7–2	Miss P. G. Stevenson.
	· 225 *Martin st.*	E.	Miss P. G. Stevenson.
205.	Waco, A.	30	
	Box 454.		Miss Mary J. Wright.

UTAH TERRITORY.

No. of Chap.	Name and Address.	No. of Mem.	Pres. and Sec.
339.	Salt Lake City, A.	6–1	Walter H. Nichols.
	Or. O. B. E. G.		Fred. E. Leonard.
487.	Salt Lake City, B.	9	Wm. W. Brown.
495.	Salt Lake City, C.	8–2	Fred. A. Stevens.
	B. G. E.		Arthur Webb.

VERMONT.

No. of Chap.	Name and Address.	No. of Mem.	Pres. and Sec.
343.	Brandon, A.	28	H. F. Copeland.
452.	Burlington, A.	4	
	253 *S. Union st.*		Harry B. Shaw.
359.	Castleton, A.	16	Miss Fannie C. Taylor.
236.	Factory Point, A.	4	Chas. L. Dench.
			Jesse D. Nichols.
508.	Middlebury, B.	4	Miss May H. Bolton.
494.	Northfield, A.	10–4	J. M. Hitt.
	B. E. Or.		Miss Clara E. Harwood.
486.	Rutland, A.	15	S. W. Merril, Z.
536.	St. Johnsbury, B.	11–1	Ozorah S. Davis.
	Box 861.	G.	Thornton B. Penfield.
613.	Winooski, A.	4–1	F. S. Paddock.
		G. M.	S. G. Ayres.

No. of Chap.	Name and Address.	No. of Mem.	Pres. and Sec.

VIRGINIA.

628.	Harrisonburg, A. Box 66.	10 G. B.	Mrs. F. A. Daingerfield. Miss M. M. Davis.
248.	Richmond, A. 302 W. Grace st.	5	Mrs. James B. Marshall.
449.	Richmond, B. 707 E. Frank st.	4 .	W. O. English.

WASHINGTON TERRITORY.

555.	Olympia, A. Thurston Co.	18	Winlock Miller. Robt. L. Blankenship.
303.	Vancouver, A.	4	Miss Julia De N. Beeson. Lawson Nicholson.

WISCONSIN.

404.	Baraboo, A.	13 E.	Noble Thompson. Miss Marie McKennan.
35.	Cedar Creek, A.	8	Dow Maxon.
42.	Columbus, A.	8	Miss F. T. Griswold.
134.	DePere, A.	18–8	Geo. T. Marston. Miss Annie S. Gilbert.
148.	DePere, B.	23–7 M. B. Z.	Miss J. White. Miss Lilian Childs.
220.	DePere, C.	16	Miss Jessie R. Jackson.
221.	DePere, D.	7	Miss Carrie Dubois.
646.	Janesville, A. Box 1644.	7	A. L. Prichard. Miss Abbie E. Prichard.
18.	Kenosha, A.	6 M. E.	Mrs. M. A. Baker. Myron E. Baker.
322.	Madison, A. 228 Langdon st.	14–4	Miss Georgie Sheldon. Andrews Allen.
524.	Milwaukee, A. 34 Prospect av.	9–4	Philip S. Abbot. Arthur E. Campbell.
344.	Monroe, A.	23–1 G.	J. J. Schindler. C. M. Craven.

No. of Mem.	Name and Address.	No. of Mem.	Pres. and Sec.
350.	Neillsville, A.	4	C. B. Bradshaw.
		E. G.	M. F. Bradshaw.
253.	Poynette, A.	2	
		B.	Harry Russell.
416.	Racine, A.	6–1	Geo. L. Ainsworth.
	926 *Main st.* Or. B. E.		J. L. McCalman.
610.	Racine, B.	5	Samuel G. Welles.
	Racine College. Or. E. G. A.		Chas. S. Lewes.
97.	St. Croix, A.	8	Ray S. Baker.
469.	West DePere, A.	15–4	A. R. DeLaney.
			Miss Margaret Ramsay.
470.	West DePere, B.	25	Miss Sara Ritchie.

FOREIGN CHAPTERS.

No. of Chap.	Name and Address.	No. of Mem.	Pres. and Sec.

CANADA.

627.	Brighton, A. Ontario.	10–2 E. O.	Miss Rose Kemp. Miss Lizzie Squier.
602.	Guelph, A. Ontario, box 213.	15–7	Miss Alice M. Petrie. Miss Daisy M. Dill.
395.	Montreal, A. 34 St. Peter st.	52–8 E.	J. J. Procter. W. D. Shaw.
451.	Sydney Mines, A. Cape Breton Island, Hill.	4 Beach E. B.	Miss I. B. Hanington. M. S. Brown.

CHILI.

441.	Valparaiso, A. Casilla, 904.	7	W. Sabina, care Rev. A. M. Merwin.

ENGLAND.

222.	London, A. Highgate, Glenggle, Wood-lane.	1–7 E. M. Or.	Lister Hayter. G. S. Hayter.
305.	London, B. 10 St. Michael's, Wood Green.	8	Miss Leila A. Mawer.
534.	London, C. 52 Tavistock sq.	5	Montague Gunning.
611.	London, D. 19 Queen's Gardens, W.	4	R. T. Walker, E.
23.	Stroud, A. Castle Bank.	26–8 B. E.	Mrs. Coley. Miss Gertrude C. Ruegg.

SCOTLAND.

475.	Dundee, A. Tayside House.	12–1 B. Or.	Miss Henderson. Miss Keiller.
549.	Linlithgow, A. Gowan Cottage.	4 B. E. G. Ost.	Wm. Wardrop, B. S.

No. of Chap.	Name and Address.	No. of Mem.	Pres. and Sec.

No. of Mem.	Name and Address.	No. of Mem.	Pres. and Sec.

No. of Chap.	Name and Address.	No. of Mem.	Pres: and Sec.

No. of Chap.	Name and Address.	No. of Mem.	Pres and Sec.

CHAPTER XVIII.

CONCLUSION.

What, after all, is our purpose in studying Nature? Is it to get for ourselves collections of rare and beautiful objects? Is it to amuse us during our leisure hours? Is it to train our powers of observation and strengthen our minds by careful discipline? Is it to satisfy our natural thirst for knowledge, and to become familiar with all the little strangers of the roadside and the wood? It is all this, but it should be much more. We ought to be learning the grand and solemn lesson that a Divine mind is showing its wisdom in every leaf and pebble, and that a Divine heart is expressing its love in every rain-drop and in every flower. This was the truth that filled the heart of him for whom our Association is named—this was the secret of his untiring zeal, and the key to his deep love of Nature. It has grown to be a pleasant custom for our chapters to celebrate Prof. Agassiz's birthday (May 28), by means of an excursion or picnic, combined with appropriate literary exercises ; and perhaps on such an occasion nothing will more truly bring home to us the sweet spirit of the great Naturalist than Whittier's poem, "The Prayer of Agassiz ;" or Longfellow's lines on his fiftieth birthday, which, by the courtesy of his publishers, we are able to reproduce.

THE FIFTIETH BIRTHDAY OF AGASSIZ.

MAY 28, 1867.

It was fifty years ago
  In the pleasant month of May,
In the beautiful Pays de Vaud,
  A child in its cradle lay.

And Nature, the old nurse, took
  The child upon her knee,
Saying: "Here is a story book
  Thy Father has written for thee."

" Come, wander with me," she said,
  "Into regions yet untrod;
And read what is still unread
  In the manuscripts of God.

And he wandered away and away
  With Nature, the dear old nurse,
Who sang to him night and day
  The rhymes of the universe.

And whenever the way seemed long,
  Or his heart began to fail,
She would sing a more wonderful song,
  Or tell a more marvellous tale.

So she keeps him still a child,
  And will not let him go,
Though at times his heart beats wild
  For the beautiful Pays de Vaud;

Though at times he hears in his dreams
  The Ranz des Vaches of old,
And the rush of mountain streams
  From glaciers clear and cold;

And the mother at home says, " Hark!
  For his voice I listen and yearn;
It is growing late and dark,
  And my boy does not return."

Requests for further information may be addressed to the President of the Association,

MR. HARLAN H. BALLARD,

Principal of Lenox Academy,

Lenox, Berkshire Co., Mass.

INDEX.